MODERN STARS

ZENDAYA

by Liz Sonneborn

Essential Library
An Imprint of Abdo Publishing
abdobooks.com

ABDOBOOKS.COM

Published by Abdo Publishing, a division of ABDO, PO Box 398166, Minneapolis, Minnesota 55439.

Printed in China.
102025
012026

Cover Photo: JC Olivera/Penske Media/Getty Images
Interior Photos: Steve Granitz/WireImage/Getty Images, 5; Andrew Toth/Getty Images for Fashion Footwear Charitable Foundation/Getty Images Entertainment/Getty Images, 8; Evan Agostini/Invision/AP Images, 12; John Salangsang/Invision for unite4:good/AP Images, 15; Jacob Boomsma/Shutterstock Images, 17; Alexandre F. Fagundes/Shutterstock Images, 20; Ed Rooney/Alamy, 22; Disney Channel/Album/Alamy, 24–25, 31; Kathy Hutchins/Shutterstock Images, 27; Jon Kopaloff/FilmMagic/Getty Images, 29; Charles Sykes/Invision/AP Images, 33, 44; Shutterstock Images, 37, 81; Tommaso Boddi/WireImage/Getty Images, 40; Columbia Pictures/Marvel Entertainment/Album/Alamy, 47; BFA/Walt Disney Studios/Alamy, 51; David M. Benett/Dave Benett Collection/WireImage/Getty Images, 52; 20th Century Fox/Album/Alamy, 54; Moviestore Collection Ltd./Alamy, 57; Eddy Chen-HBO/PictureLux/The Hollywood Archive/Alamy, 59, 61; Photo12/7e Art/Matt Kennedy/Columbia Pictures/Marvel Studios/Alamy, 63; Clint Spaulding/WWD/Penske Media/Getty Images, 66; Legendary Entertainment/Warner Bros./Album/Alamy, 69; Daniele Venturelli/WireImage/Getty Images, 70; Little Lamb/The Reasonable Bunch/Album/Alamy, 76; Invision for the Television Academy/AP Images, 79; Stefania D'Alessandro/Getty Images Entertainment/Getty Images, 83; Cindy Ord/Getty Images for SiriusXM/Getty Images Entertainment/Getty Images, 85; Kevin Winter/Getty Images Entertainment/Getty Images, 88; Hoda Davaine/Dave Benett Collection/WireImage/Getty Images, 91; Loredana Sangiuliano/Shutterstock Images, 96; John Shearer/WireImage/Getty Images, 98

Editor: Laura Stickney
Series Designer: Karli Hughes

Library of Congress Control Number: 2025939175

PUBLISHER'S CATALOGING-IN-PUBLICATION DATA

Names: Sonneborn, Liz, author.
Title: Zendaya / by Liz Sonneborn
Description: Minneapolis, Minnesota: Abdo Publishing, 2026 | Series: Modern stars | Includes online resources and index.
Identifiers: ISBN 9781098298142 (lib. bdg.) | ISBN 9798384931942 (ebook)
Subjects: LCSH: Zendaya, 1996--Juvenile literature. | Actresses--United States--Biography--Juvenile literature. | Motion picture actors and actresses--United States--Biography--Juvenile literature. | Women singers--United States--Biography--Juvenile literature.
Classification: DDC 782.42164--dc23

CONTENTS

CHAPTER ONE

BECOMING ZENDAYA

On February 22, 2015, 18-year-old actress Zendaya confidently walked down the red carpet at the Academy Awards, also known as the Oscars, in Los Angeles, California. She was wearing an elegant white satin dress with off-the-shoulder straps, along with dangling pearl earrings and a shimmering cuff bracelet. But Zendaya's most notable style choice was her hairstyle. Her hair was fashioned into long dreadlocks that fell nearly to her waist.

Hoping to get Zendaya to look their way, photographers shouted out, "Zendaya, right here on the left, please" and "Up top, sweetheart." One of them, however, simply blurted out what

Zendaya's red-carpet appearance at the 2015 Academy Awards marked her first time attending the prestigious event. She has since attended multiple times. >>

other onlookers were likely thinking: "You look gorgeous, Zendaya!"[1]

Zendaya's appearance on the red carpet was brief. But the Oscar moment proved a turning point in her career. Within only a few years, Zendaya would rise to international fame, becoming one of the most acclaimed stars of her generation.

Before the 2015 Oscars, Zendaya had already had plenty of red-carpet experience. For years, she had worked with stylist Law Roach. Stylists help celebrities choose clothing and accessories for events. They may also negotiate with fashion design houses to borrow expensive items for their celebrity clients to wear. In turn, designers get free publicity when the press photographs a celebrity wearing their clothes.

Zendaya seemed like a perfect candidate for designer giveaways. Standing five feet, ten inches (178 cm) tall, the actress's height and frame made her well suited for modeling designer dresses.[2] But Roach often had a hard time persuading designers to offer Zendaya any pieces. As a teenage star on the Disney Channel show *K. C. Undercover,* Zendaya's fan base was mostly tweens—hardly natural customers for luxury designer brands. But Roach was not above badgering fashion houses until they relented. He knew that in the end, designers were sure to be pleased by how Zendaya modeled their clothes.

THE SINGLE-NAME CLUB

Zendaya's father was responsible for her uncommon name. Pronounced *zen-DAY-ah*, it was inspired by the name Tendai. This means "to give thanks" in the language of the Shona people of southern Africa. Zendaya explained that her dad tweaked the African name to *Zendaya* because he "had a thing for Zs and Zen."[3] The distinctiveness of the name helped Zendaya become one of the rare celebrities, such as Cher and Madonna, who are known by only one name.

A STYLE STAR

Under normal circumstances, Zendaya was unlikely to get an invitation to the 2015 Academy Awards. The event was meant to highlight the elite of the film industry, and Zendaya was the star of a children's television show who had never been in a movie before. The young actress was able to attend the awards only by chance. An agent she knew happened to have an extra ticket and invited her.

Determined to make the most of the opportunity, Zendaya worked with Roach to craft an eye-catching look. The stylist managed to snag a beautiful dress from designer Vivienne Westwood. Its style and shape resembled the glamorous gowns that Hollywood stars often wore in the 1930s and 1940s. Other stylists might have paired the dress with a retro hairstyle, but Zendaya and Roach wanted to try something different. Their choice of long dreadlocks was unexpected and gave Zendaya's look a modern touch. Since dreadlocks are associated with Afro-Caribbean culture, Zendaya's hairstyle was also a nod to her and Roach's shared Black heritage.

The complicated hairstyle took many hours to get right. After putting in all that effort, Zendaya was going to make sure people noticed her look. She didn't have formal permission to walk the red carpet at the Academy Awards. But by exuding a confidence that made people think she belonged there, Zendaya was able to sneak onto the carpet and pose for the photographers. The strategy paid off even more than Zendaya had hoped. She was featured in Oscar fashion

Zendaya's partnership with stylist Law Roach began in 2011, when the actress was just 14 years old. The pair attended a fashion event together in 2016.

roundups in magazines such as *The Hollywood Reporter* and *Entertainment Weekly*, appearing alongside A-list movie stars. Zendaya was also singled out in a post on the website of *Vogue*, a leading American fashion magazine.

The post was titled "Zendaya Is This Academy Awards' Breakout Style Star." It declared, "Oh, what a difference a serious red-carpet moment can make!" The writer of the post said Zendaya's outfit was "all very grown up (which is to say, all very un-Disney)." This was exactly what a child star hoping to be recognized as a serious actress wanted to achieve. The piece concluded, "We'll be keeping our eye on you, Zendaya."[4]

SPEAKING HER MIND

The night after the Oscars, Zendaya watched fashion commentary on the television show *Fashion Police*, which aired on the E! network. The show featured fashion reporters, who commented on red-carpet looks and often made cruel jokes about fashion mistakes to take celebrities down a peg. Cohost Giuliana Rancic critiqued Zendaya's appearance at the Academy Awards, complaining that her hairstyle overpowered her small frame.

Rancic added, "I feel like she smells like patchouli oil." This was a reference to a fragrance associated with hippies of the 1960s and 1970s. From offscreen, someone shouted, "Or weed," making Rancic laugh and say, "Yeah, maybe weed."[5]

> **"I don't just sing, dance, and act because I love it. You have to have a purpose, and mine is to connect with the world, to get across messages that are important."[7]**
>
> —Zendaya, 2016

Zendaya was so full of rage that she screamed at the television. Insulted and hurt, she immediately thought about making mean remarks about Rancic on social media. Instead, Zendaya calmed down and went to her room to gather her thoughts. Her parents were teachers, and they had taught her the importance of making reasoned arguments to communicate ideas. She spent hours researching and crafting a response, which she posted on her Instagram profile.

"There is a fine line between what is funny and disrespectful," Zendaya's statement began. She then pointed out that saying a young woman wearing dreadlocks must smell of marijuana was both "a large stereotype" and "outrageously offensive."[6] She explained that many of her family members, as well as numerous prominent Black Americans such as film director Ava DuVernay, wore dreadlocks, and none of them smelled of marijuana.

Zendaya went on to say that many Americans are prejudiced against people of color who sport natural hairstyles such as dreadlocks, and that was precisely why she had worn the hairstyle to the Oscars. "My wearing my hair in locs on an Oscar red carpet was to showcase them in a positive light, to remind people of color that our hair is good enough," Zendaya explained. "To me locs are a symbol of strength and beauty, almost like a lion's mane."[8]

Zendaya's thoughtful statement spread rapidly across the internet and drew widespread praise. Many Black American women, including celebrated actresses Kerry Washington and Viola Davis, were particularly grateful for her remarks. Washington posted, "Well done Beautiful. XO," while Davis declared, "I celebrate you sis!"[9] Media reports further spread Zendaya's statement, prompting a national conversation about natural hairstyles and the prejudices against them.

ENDING HAIR DISCRIMINATION

In 2024, Law Roach credited Zendaya's 2015 Oscar look with raising awareness about hair-related discrimination against people of color. He speculated that together, he and Zendaya had helped to increase the acceptance of dreadlocks, braids, and other natural hairstyles. Since Zendaya's Oscars appearance, several states have adopted laws that ban hair-related discrimination in workplaces and schools.

In response, Rancic quickly taped a segment that aired on *E! News* that evening. She explained, "I want to say to Zendaya, and anyone else out there that I have hurt, that I am so, so sincerely sorry."[10] In a Twitter post, Zendaya said she appreciated Rancic's sentiments, adding, "I hope that others negatively affected by her words can also find it in their hearts to accept her apology."[11]

GLAMOROUS AND RELATABLE

Some young actresses in Zendaya's situation might have remained quiet after the insult, fearing a backlash. But Zendaya felt an obligation to speak out. Her passionate response ended up bolstering her career rather than hurting it. Her young fan base came to respect her even more, while the incident brought Zendaya to the attention of many adults. For new admirers of Zendaya, the first impression

Zendaya's bold looks, such as the armor-inspired gown she wore to the 2018 Met Gala, have cemented her status as a fashion icon.

A BARBIE FOR ZENDAYA

Executives at the Mattel toy company, which sells Barbie dolls, saw Zendaya as a role model for girls because of the way she stood up for herself and her culture. They made the actress a one-of-a-kind Barbie doll dressed in a replica of her 2015 Oscar look. The doll had accurate details and even included the ring on Zendaya's pinky finger. On Instagram, Zendaya changed her profile picture to a headshot of the doll and wrote, "When I was little I couldn't find a Barbie that looked like me, my . . . how times have changed."[12]

she made during the controversy highlighted two aspects that have since endeared her to fans worldwide. Zendaya's red-carpet look showed off her glamorous and charismatic persona, while her Instagram statement revealed her thoughtful, compassionate side. As the face of luxury brands, Zendaya can seem cool, alluring, and perfect. But when playing the wisecracking teen MJ in the Spider-Man franchise or the troubled Rue in the TV show *Euphoria*, Zendaya seems like someone whom viewers might know in real life.

On social media, the actress continues to share photographs of her fabulous outfits alongside frank discussions of social issues. Throughout her career, Zendaya has managed to intrigue fans by seeming sophisticated yet relatable, and unknowable yet familiar. This fascinating combination has helped propel her to the top of the fashion and entertainment worlds.

CHAPTER TWO

GROWING UP

Zendaya Maree Stoermer Coleman was born to Kazembe Ajamu Coleman and Claire Stoermer on September 1, 1996. In a 2015 public service announcement celebrating Immigrant Heritage Month, Zendaya sat between her parents and shared how her name reflects her ethnic roots. Zendaya is derived from an African name—a nod to her father's heritage. Maree is a common African spelling of the French name Marie, which is her mother's middle name. Stoermer is her mother's German surname.

Both names reflect Zendaya's European roots through her mother's lineage. "I literally have . . . a timeline in history in my name," Zendaya explained. "I am from Africa as well as from Germany, and I am very proud of that."[1]

Zendaya credits her parents with teaching her the values of humility and hard work. >>

A DEVOTED GRANDMOTHER

Zendaya considers her paternal grandmother one of the greatest "sheroes" in her life. Despite her busy schedule, Zendaya frequently called her grandmother on the phone, explaining that "hearing her voice is like food for the soul."[2] One of Zendaya's biggest fans, her grandmother had a display of magazine covers on which Zendaya appears in the bedroom of her Oakland home. She also followed Zendaya's every move online, so much so that Zendaya said her grandmother knew her schedule better than she did herself. Zendaya's grandmother passed away in 2025.

Growing up in Oakland, California, Zendaya was always surrounded by family. Her father had three daughters, Katianna, Annabella, and Kaylee, and two sons, Austin and Julien, from a previous marriage. All five of Zendaya's half siblings are much older than her, and many of their children are Zendaya's age or older. This meant that when Zendaya was born, she was already an aunt. She has long been known as Auntie Daya to her many nieces and nephews.

A DIVERSE COMMUNITY

Zendaya enjoyed her childhood in Oakland. The northern California city is one of the most diverse cities in the United States. Its history is closely intertwined with the civil rights movement. Some of that history was made in the house in which the actress grew up. Her father and his

Oakland is located in the East Bay region of California's San Francisco Bay Area. Zendaya attended the city's Oakland School for the Arts.

seven siblings were raised in the same house. In the 1960s, the Black Panther Party, a Black political activist group, was founded in Oakland. One reason it formed was to protect Black residents from assaults by the police. Several of Zendaya's aunts were members of the party, and the organization sometimes held meetings in the basement of her family home.

As a biracial child, Zendaya began thinking about racial issues from a young age. Both her parents were teachers. Her father taught physical education at a private school with mostly white students. Zendaya attended this school. Her mother taught at an underfunded public school in an impoverished Black neighborhood. Zendaya spent afternoons tutoring students in reading at her mother's school. She was struck by how few resources the public facility had compared with her private school.

As one of only a few Black students at her school, Zendaya sometimes found herself in uncomfortable situations. One day, she went to school with straightened hair. When her white classmates complimented her new hairstyle, Zendaya realized they liked it only because it made her look more like a white girl. She later recalled that the incident made her feel weird.

Another incident from Zendaya's youth stuck with her as she grew older. On New Year's Day in 2009, a young Black man named Oscar Grant was shot and killed by a police officer at a train station. The incident occurred near the school where her mother worked. The killing outraged Oakland residents, some of whom rioted in the streets. Grant's death was later dramatized in the 2013 film *Fruitvale Station*, one of Zendaya's favorite movies.

COMING OUT OF HER SHELL

When Zendaya was a young child, her parents worried about her extreme shyness. She would often retreat into herself and not interact with other children. Her parents decided to have Zendaya repeat kindergarten, hoping the extra year would help her catch up to her peers socially.

In middle school, Zendaya also struggled with anxiety. Once, when taking a test, she was so worried about getting a good grade that she had a panic attack. Her teacher had to take her out into the hall and tell her to take deep breaths to calm down.

Despite these troubles, Zendaya was a good and confident student. She sometimes got in trouble with teachers because she insisted on taking over group projects. She recalled telling her fellow students, "You guys are going to mess it up, so don't worry, I'll do everything."[3]

BECOMING A VEGETARIAN

When Zendaya was 11 years old, she was on a road trip with her father when they drove by a large building. Zendaya's father explained that it was a slaughterhouse. It was the first time Zendaya really thought about meat coming from slaughtered animals. That day, she vowed to become a vegetarian, although she admits that the diet is sometimes difficult for her. Zendaya has said that she decided to become a vegetarian because she loves animals, not because she loves vegetables.

This confidence led Zendaya to embrace acting, which helped her overcome her shyness. Her first acting role was in an elementary school play based on the children's book *James and the Giant Peach*. She had a nonspeaking part as a silkworm. "I killed it," Zendaya later said. "I was reacting

As a young actor, Zendaya appeared in several local theater productions, including some at San Francisco's American Conservatory Theater.

and giving face, and I was the best dang silkworm there ever was."[4]

Zendaya's eagerness to take charge led her to persuade her elementary school principal to let her and two other Black students perform a play for Black History Month. She took on the role of Bessie Coleman, a pioneering Black pilot, while her friends played abolitionist Harriet Tubman and businesswoman Madam C. J. Walker. Zendaya was aware that many of her white classmates knew little about Black American historical figures. She later said she "just felt we needed to raise awareness about the importance of these women."[5]

Young Zendaya also embraced expressing herself through fashion. Standing six feet, four inches (193 cm), Zendaya's mother is so tall that she has trouble finding clothes that fit.[6] She enjoyed playing with fashion by choosing outfits for her daughter, who appreciated the attention.

Zendaya soon began to develop her own sense of style by dressing up in clothes she found in her grandmothers' closets. Her paternal grandmother taught her how to put on makeup. Zendaya enjoyed putting outfits together, applying makeup, and taking pictures of herself posing as if she was at a magazine photo shoot.

DISCOVERING ACTING

Zendaya was exposed to professional theater through her mother, who was the house manager for the California Shakespeare Theater. For many summers, Zendaya hung out backstage, watching the actors rehearse. She had a ritual before each performance of visiting the food stand, where the staff knew to bring her favorite meal—a veggie burrito, a chocolate chip cookie, and a bottle of juice. While eating, Zendaya would sit back and watch whatever

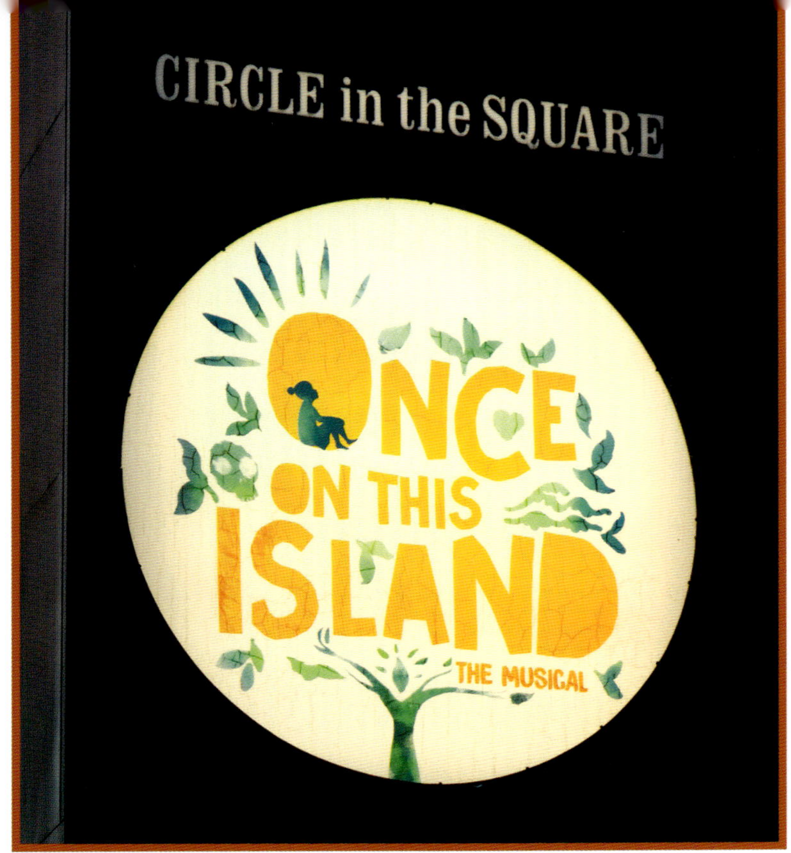

In 2009, 13-year-old Zendaya played the role of Little Ti Moune in *Once on This Island*. The musical tells the story of a young girl on a Caribbean island.

play was being performed that night. "I was that weird eight-year-old who was into Shakespeare," she later said.[7]

With her parents' encouragement, Zendaya began to study acting and dance. She performed with a local hip-hop dance troupe called Future Shock and studied hula dancing at the Academy of Hawaiian Arts in Oakland. She also began auditioning for regional theater productions, winning a starring role in the musical *Once on This Island* at the Berkeley Playhouse.

As she got older, Zendaya branched out into modeling. She modeled for clothing stores such as

Old Navy and Macy's. One of her most notable gigs was a music video–style television commercial for the department store Sears. She was one of several young dancers backing up Disney Channel star Selena Gomez as Gomez sang a song titled "I'm Gonna Arrive."

By age 13, Zendaya was sure she wanted to become a professional entertainer. Knowing her options were limited in northern California, she told her parents she wanted to move to Los Angeles. Zendaya later recalled, "Luckily I had parents who were like, 'You know what? We believe in you.'"[8] Her mother stayed in Oakland, working two jobs to keep the family afloat, while her father quit his job to move to Los Angeles with Zendaya. The aspiring entertainer was determined to make all her Hollywood dreams come true.

BEYONCÉ FAN

When Zendaya was growing up, pop music superstar Beyoncé was her idol. She had a poster of Beyoncé on her wall and celebrated her thirteenth birthday by attending one of the singer's concerts. Just seven years later, Zendaya appeared in the music video for "All Night," a song on Beyoncé's album *Lemonade*. Zendaya called the experience "one of the most beautiful things I've ever had the honor of being [a part] of."[9]

CHAPTER THREE

A DISNEY KID

During her first months in Los Angeles, Zendaya struggled to adjust to her new life. She and her father lived in a cramped downtown apartment, and she missed her friends and relatives back home. Zendaya particularly regretted being so far away from her mother when she got her first period because her father did not know how to help her.

As she went to auditions, Zendaya faced open hostility from some of the other child actors she met. Many of them had been in the entertainment industry for years and did not appreciate having to compete with a talented newcomer. In Zendaya's words, "There was this kind of energy, particularly among the other girls, of, like, 'Oooh, I'm going to get you.'"[1]

Soon, Zendaya attracted the attention of a talent manager from Disney Channel. At the time, this

In the TV show *Shake It Up*, Zendaya's character, Rocky, is smart, studious, and shy. Bella Thorne's character, CeCe, is more rebellious and outspoken. >>

24-hour television cable channel was available in almost 100 million American homes.[2] It produced a variety of live-action programs for children and teens, many of which were geared toward tween girls. Its most successful programs included the series *Hannah Montana* and the *High School Musical* original movies.

The channel's strategy was to develop narratives that appealed to tween girls while casting young female celebrities with whom tween girls could identify. Disney Channel heavily promoted these celebrities in crossover projects. These included concerts, made-for-television films, and public appearances.

SHAKING IT UP

In 2010, Disney Channel set out to produce *Shake It Up*, a comedy series starring two girls. The casting department thought 14-year-old Zendaya's screen presence made her the perfect fit for one of the lead roles. A senior vice president of casting told the press, "She's smart, confident, and completely engaging. She's somebody you never tire of watching."[3]

Shake It Up follows the adventures of two best friends living in Chicago, Illinois. Zendaya plays Raquel "Rocky" Blue, while costar Bella Thorne portrays

Zendaya and her *Shake It Up* castmates performed live at the D23 Expo in 2011. They danced to the Selena Gomez song "Shake It Up Remix."

Cecelia "CeCe" Jones. Rocky and CeCe are cast in a local teen dance television show. The series follows the backstage intrigue on the show and the girls' lives at home and at school.

By the time she was cast in *Shake It Up*, Thorne was an experienced actress who had had recurring roles in half a dozen television series. Although Zendaya was new to television, her dance training gave her a leg up on Thorne who, before the show, had never taken a dance class. First airing on November 7, 2010, *Shake It Up* was an instant hit. More than six million viewers watched the pilot.[4] By the following June, it was the number one television series with children ages six to 11 and tweens ages nine to 14.[5]

FASHION AND MUSIC

As a rising Disney Channel star, Zendaya was required to make public appearances to promote the show. She had to attend many events that featured red carpets. She attended her first movie premiere wearing clothes she bought from Target. She later recalled that she felt cool in the outfit.

But Zendaya's father realized that going forward, his daughter would need help putting together red-carpet looks. He had a friend who knew Law Roach, the owner of a vintage clothing store in Chicago. He suggested that Roach could help dress Zendaya for the premiere of *Never Say Never*, a documentary about the pop sensation Justin Bieber.

Roach took Zendaya to Kitson, a trendy local department store, and

FIRST (ON-SCREEN) KISS

In one *Shake It Up* episode, Zendaya was supposed to kiss an actor on the lips. But she was hesitant to do so. She had not yet kissed a boy in real life and did not want something as intimate as her first kiss to be caught on camera and broadcast to an audience. While filming, Zendaya took charge of the scene and kissed her scene partner on the cheek rather than on the lips.

picked out a green patent leather miniskirt and a shimmering silver blazer. Zendaya loved the youthful yet sophisticated combination. Roach began dressing the young actress regularly, earning her trust as he encouraged her to experiment with fashion.

Zendaya also experimented with her style in music videos. When she started working for Disney Channel, she hoped the company would help her develop her musical talents, as it had done for many of its earlier teen performers. These included Britney Spears, Justin Timberlake, Miley Cyrus, and Selena Gomez.

In 2011, Disney released a music video for Zendaya's song "Dig Down Deeper," a girl power anthem that appeared on the soundtrack for the animated Disney Channel movie *Pixie Hollow Games.* Several songs that Zendaya performed on

At the 2011 *Never Say Never* premiere, Zendaya accessorized her outfit with a silver necklace and black tights. Roach's styling strategies helped Zendaya attract attention early in her career.

Shake It Up were also included on soundtrack albums associated with the show. Her duet "Watch Me" with Bella Thorne appeared on the *Billboard* Hot 100. This chart tracks the 100 most popular songs in the United States. Another notable *Shake It Up* song was "Fashion Is My Kryptonite," which Zendaya and Thorne performed on a special episode of the show titled "Made in Japan." While singing the song, the actresses modeled dozens of red-carpet outfits.

In late 2012, Zendaya signed a contract with Hollywood Records, Disney's music company. The following year saw the release of her studio album *Zendaya*, which included the hit single "Replay." The song rose to No. 40 on the *Billboard* Hot 100 and eventually earned platinum certification by selling more than one million copies.[6] Zendaya's singing career was

WORST LOOK

Not every outfit Law Roach picked out for Zendaya has been a winner. In 2023, *Elle* magazine asked Zendaya to name her worst fashion mistake. She immediately had an answer. Eleven years earlier, during Zendaya's first press tour for *Shake It Up*, Roach dressed her in an aqua blazer, a salmon-and-white striped cardigan, and a yellow undershirt. Zendaya joked that she's still angry with Roach for dressing her in the outfit.

bolstered by the Swag It Out Tour, during which she performed at arenas and state fairs from 2012 to 2014.

BUSY WITH DISNEY

During her three seasons on *Shake It Up*, Zendaya was also busy with other Disney Channel side projects. In 2011, she was a host of *Make Your Mark: Ultimate Dance Off—Shake It Up Edition*. This was a Disney Channel dance contest for young children and tweens.

The following year, Zendaya and Thorne appeared in the television movie *Frenemies*, in which they play two teens competing to be the editor of a web magazine called *Geekly Chic*. The rivals end up becoming best friends. Zendaya later appeared in *Zapped*, a 2014 Disney Channel movie about a teen girl who finds a dog-training app that allows her to control badly behaving male relatives and classmates.

But Zendaya's most high-profile side project was *Dancing with the Stars*, a televised dance competition in which

In the 2014 film *Zapped*, Zendaya plays a 16-year-old girl named Zoey Stevens.

famous entertainers and athletes are paired with professional dancers. In early 2013, Zendaya appeared as a contestant on season 16 of the popular show, which then aired on ABC, a network owned by the same parent company as Disney Channel. At the time, Zendaya was the youngest star to ever appear on the program.

Zendaya was partnered with dancer Valentin "Val" Chmerkovskiy, who was initially upset by the pairing. Zendaya's height was one concern because Chmerkovskiy preferred working with shorter dancers. Her age was another problem. Chmerkovskiy was known for adding a sexy vibe to his performances, which would have been inappropriate with a teenage partner.

Chmerkovskiy also assumed that because Zendaya was a child actor, she would not take the competition seriously. Chmerkovskiy made it clear that they were going to practice every step over and over until it was perfect, which suited the perfectionist in Zendaya just fine. She said, "With Val, he's like the perfect balance between tough and nice."[7]

From the beginning, Zendaya and Chmerkovskiy earned high scores from the judges. But it wasn't until week eight of the show that they received tens from all three judges—their first perfect score. The partners'

Dancing with the Stars finalists Zendaya and Val Chmerkovskiy performed on the TV show *Good Morning America* in 2013.

winning streak continued into the finale, during which they were awarded all perfect scores. Zendaya and Chmerkovskiy finished the competition with a judges' score of 95 points. This was one point above the score of their closest competitors, country singer Kellie Pickler and her partner Derek Hough.[8]

Viewers then had the chance to vote for their favorite teams. The audience's scores were combined with the judges' scores to determine the final result. Preferred by the public, Pickler and Hough ended up winning the first-place trophy, and Zendaya and Chmerkovskiy came in second. However, this outcome was not without controversy. Due to a technical glitch, votes cast on ABC's website were not counted in the total. Because Zendaya's young fans were the most likely to vote online, there was speculation that the last-minute glitch was the reason Zendaya lost the competition.

ASSESSING HER EARLY DISNEY YEARS

Characteristically, Zendaya took her *Dancing with the Stars* loss in stride, telling the press, "I'm very proud. I'm very happy and I get to leave here with an amazing experience."[9] But years later, she reassessed her time on the show and acknowledged the emotional toll it took on her. In a January 2025 interview with *W* magazine, she confessed, "I'm still harboring a little animosity about that. I felt that loss."[10]

As an adult, Zendaya realized that she had been too young for such a high-pressure situation. "I was only 16 years old, and it was highly stressful," she said. "Being on live television every week? It's so scary."[11]

Zendaya also came to regret the limited education she had received as a working teen. The *Shake It Up* set had a small classroom where the young actors were expected to work with tutors. But Zendaya observed that some of her peers just cheated their way through online school programs. As teachers, her parents urged Disney Channel to hire a skilled, demanding tutor for Zendaya, who was equally intent on getting the best education she could under the circumstances.

But with no time off, the young actress was exhausted. She tried to do schoolwork in cars, planes, and hotel rooms. In a 2024 interview with tennis star Serena Williams, Zendaya sadly admitted that she wished she had gone to school.

In the same interview, Zendaya acknowledged the pressure she faced while working on *Shake It Up*. "I felt like I was thrust into a very adult position," she said. "I was becoming the breadwinner of my family very early."[12]

BETWEEN U AND ME

In 2013, the Disney-owned publishing company Hyperion Books released *Between U and Me: How to Rock Your Tween Years with Style and Confidence*. This self-help book was coauthored by Zendaya and writer Sheryl Berk. In the book, the star offered advice on fashion, friends, family, aspirations, and other topics relevant to tween readers. The book was inspired by questions young fans asked Zendaya on her social media accounts.

She also felt burdened by the pressure to be perfect and live up to the expectations that others had of her. Many child actors experience similar pressures and may try to cope through drug and alcohol use or other behaviors. But Zendaya took a different path. She became determined to take control of her career and her life.

CHAPTER FOUR

TAKING THE REINS

In late 2013, as the third and final season of *Shake It Up* was winding down, Zendaya sat in a meeting room with a group of Disney Channel executives. They were all eager to stay in business with Zendaya, who had proved to be one of their most popular and versatile stars. The executives were developing what they thought was a perfect follow-up Disney Channel show for her—*Super Awesome Katy.*

This action-comedy series would focus on a girl named Katy. She would discover that her parents were international spies. She would join them in the family business, all while being an otherwise normal teenager navigating the world of high school.

Zendaya's *K. C. Undercover* costars described the young actress as driven and goal oriented. They admired her ability to handle both comedic and dramatic moments on the show. >>

NOON

After Zendaya's childhood dog Midnight died in 2015, a friend gave her a puppy. Zendaya named him Afternoon, or Noon for short. Since then, the actress has been devoted to the black miniature schnauzer, calling him her "kid." For years, Noon has been Zendaya's constant companion, visiting all her television and movie sets. Zendaya credits Noon with keeping her sane whenever her busy schedule gets too crazy or exhausting. Like his famous owner, Noon is a social media star. He has almost 43,000 followers on Instagram.[3]

Many young performers would jump at such an offer. But 16-year-old Zendaya told the executives they would have to make considerable changes if she was to sign on to the project. The title itself made her bristle. She said, "The title is whack. That's gonna change. Do I look like a Katy to you?"[1] Katy became K. C. Cooper, and the show's title was changed to *K. C. Undercover.*

Zendaya also said that she did not want her character to be a singer, actress, or dancer, as so many female lead characters were on Disney Channel shows. Instead of a typical cool girl, she wanted to play a character who was bookish, socially awkward, and excellent at math and martial arts. On television, these skills were more typically associated with boys than girls. Zendaya thought it was important for her fans to see a girl in what she called a "guy role," so that both boys and girls "can look up to a girl and say, 'I want to be like this girl.'"[2]

Zendaya was upset about the severe lack of diversity on Disney Channel shows too. She insisted that Black actors play her character's family members, so that Black American kids could see people on television who looked like them and their relatives. She later explained, "A lot of people who aren't people of color can't quite understand what it's like to grow up and not see yourself in mainstream media."[4]

> **"A lot of people don't realize their power. I have so many friends who say yes to everything or feel like they can't stand up for themselves in a situation. No: You *have* the power."[5]**
>
> **—Zendaya, 2017**

BEING K.C.

Zendaya's final demand was the most important. She wanted to be not only the series' star but also its producer. Being a producer would allow her to have a say about the show's plotlines and to oversee its day-to-day operations. During the negotiations, Zendaya made it clear that she was willing to walk away if Disney Channel refused her demands. Rather than lose their star, the executives agreed to everything she asked for, including the producer role.

As a producer, Zendaya had many ideas about how to improve the Disney Channel formula. She advised making the show's lighting less bright and the actors' clothes less showy. She also wanted to tone down the acting style, which she thought was too over the top in many Disney Channel shows.

A teen joining a spy organization was an outlandish premise. But Zendaya still wanted the show to feel somewhat realistic. For example, if her character woke up in the middle of the night, Zendaya didn't want her to be wearing matching pajamas and perfect makeup.

K. C. Undercover had a three-season run.[6] In 2016, 2017, and 2019, Zendaya's portrayal of K. C. won her the Kids' Choice Award for Favorite Female TV Star. On the show's set, Zendaya also met Darnell Appling, who has since become her personal assistant and close friend.

Zendaya appeared onstage at the 2017 Kids' Choice Awards in Los Angeles, California. She accepted an award for her performance in *K. C. Undercover*.

ON THE SIDE

During the first season of *K. C. Undercover*, Zendaya began working on a new album with Hollywood Records. She saw her first album as a "baby step in the right direction," but she had higher hopes for the second one. In her eyes, the *Zendaya* album was "pop with a touch of R&B." She wanted her new album to sound like "R&B with a touch of pop," believing that would appeal more to older teens.[7]

Public anticipation for Zendaya's latest project grew after it was announced that she was teaming up with superstar producer Timbaland on some of the album's tracks. In 2016, one single, "Something New," was released. But ultimately, Zendaya's second album was shelved with no explanation from her or the record company. Whatever happened behind the scenes seemed to embitter Zendaya toward the music industry. In a 2019 interview, she said, "I think

A HEAD FOR BUSINESS

When Zendaya first started acting, she did not take much interest in the business side of the entertainment industry, although her parents forced her to read all her contracts. But she soon came to see that only by understanding contracts could she be sure she was being treated fairly. Zendaya has said her most important advice for aspiring performers is to "look over those contracts, every single word, and don't sign anything that isn't worth it to you."[8]

the industry takes a little bit of passion away from you. It sucks you dry a little bit."[9]

Zendaya took on another side project in 2016, when she announced her Daya by Zendaya clothing line. It was a collaboration between Zendaya and Law Roach. Zendaya insisted that the brand offer affordable clothes in a variety of sizes. She was inspired by her very tall mother, who struggles to find clothes that fit.

Many items in the line were unisex. This was because Zendaya recalled that when her parents let her pick out her own clothes as a kid, she often found what she wanted in the boys' section. Despite Zendaya's promotion of Daya, she cut ties with the brand's company in 2018 after hearing about customer service complaints.

With Roach by her side, Zendaya continued refining her style in her late teens. She and Roach constantly bounced ideas off one another, exchanging images that inspired them. These ranged from old fashion photos of celebrities such as Cher and Bianca Jagger to shots of stylish people walking down the street.

Zendaya and Roach also created characters associated with each outfit. Zendaya could play these characters as she modeled clothes on the red carpet. As she explained, "It's an odd thing to get up in front of people and pose in a crazy outfit. For me, if I create a character, it makes it feel less strange."[10] Before events, Zendaya started practicing poses in the mirror to see which ones worked best.

Roach encouraged Zendaya to try fashion-forward looks, such as a black-and-teal gown from the fashion house Ungaro. Zendaya wore it at the 2014 Grammy Awards. Fausto Puglisi, Ungaro's creative director, was so pleased with how Zendaya modeled the dress that he got her an invitation to the 2015 Met Gala. This is an annual fundraiser for the Costume Institute at the Metropolitan Museum of Art in New York City.

Overseen by *Vogue* magazine's editor-in-chief Anna Wintour, the Met Gala is the premier event of the US fashion industry. Each year, the gala has a different theme. Attendees, many of whom are celebrities, are expected to dress in a way that expresses the theme.

SECRET BOYFRIEND

During Zendaya's teen years, fans on social media constantly speculated about whom she might be dating. Rumors spread that she was involved with actor Trevor Jackson, but they both claimed they were only close friends. In 2017, Zendaya finally came clean about her first love in a *Vogue* interview. Without naming names, she explained that as a teen, she had been in a four-year relationship. It had ended in early 2016 when her boyfriend broke up with her. Zendaya took the breakup well. Instead of fretting about what she had done wrong, she learned from the experience and moved on.

Zendaya paired her dramatic 2015 Met Gala dress with a golden crown, black heels, and cuff bracelets. The actress told reporters that she liked the gown's fun, youthful quality.

In 2015, the theme was "China: Through the Looking Glass," and Zendaya wowed the gala with her Puglisi gown. It featured a black halter top and a short red skirt with bejeweled sun patterns and a long train. Zendaya has since been a frequent Met Gala attendee, with fashionistas eagerly waiting to see what she will wear each year.

ON SOCIAL MEDIA

During the controversy surrounding her dreadlocks in 2015, Zendaya learned that fashion had the power to get people talking. The incident also made her realize that her popularity on social media could be an impactful tool.

"As my social platforms grew," Zendaya explained, "I realized that my voice was so much more important than I originally thought."[11]

Zendaya began using her social media accounts to share ideas about race, equality, diversity, and other topics. For instance, she showed support for football player Colin Kaepernick's protests against racial injustice. She also shared her knowledge of Black historical figures, posting about the topic so often that she joked she was becoming a professor of Black history.

On her birthday, Zendaya used social media to raise money for important causes. When she turned 18, she called on her 19 million Instagram followers to contribute to a fund to feed 150 students in developing countries for a year.[12] On her nineteenth birthday, Zendaya asked fans to contribute money to help buy a home for three South African brothers whose parents had died of AIDS.

She had met the boys while serving as an ambassador for a United Nations organization combating the spread of HIV, the virus that causes AIDS. Zendaya spoke about using her status to advance change. She said, "If I can make it cool for young people to buy a certain handbag, maybe I can make it cool to be safe, protect yourself, get tested—to love yourself."[13]

CHAPTER FIVE

BREAKOUT

As Zendaya entered her second year of *K. C. Undercover*, she began to think about what to do next. She was aging out of her Disney Channel career and feared that her association with children's television shows would keep casting directors from seeing her as a serious actress. Zendaya was getting plenty of offers, but nothing seemed good enough. "I wanted to do quality projects, cool things that made me excited," she explained.[1]

Zendaya was also worried that as a Black actress, her opportunities would be limited. She told her manager to send her to auditions even if the part she was auditioning for was a white character. She said, "Let me get in the room. Maybe they'll change their minds."[2]

In *Spider-Man: Homecoming*, Zendaya's character Michelle "MJ" Jones is known for being a bookish, awkward, and snarky loner. >>

PLAYING MJ

Finally, Zendaya heard about a part that really excited her. It was the role of MJ, a high school friend of Peter Parker, or Spider-Man, in *Spider-Man: Homecoming*. This was the first movie in a reboot of the Marvel Studios *Spider-Man* franchise. In the script, MJ was a smart outsider who always had a book in her hand and a sarcastic comeback on her lips. Zendaya liked the character because she was a little weird. She later said, "I like that [MJ's] different, and I think a lot of young people—especially young women—can relate to that."[3]

SPIDER-MAN FAN

Zendaya was not a big comic book fan growing up, but Spider-Man was always her favorite superhero. As she explained, "He's just a kid . . . trying to balance living life and being a teenager . . . while also like doing the most outrageous things."[4] Zendaya was also a big fan of *The Amazing Spider-Man*, a 2012 film from an earlier version of the *Spider-Man* franchise. The movie starred Andrew Garfield and Emma Stone. The film had a special meaning for Zendaya because she saw it on her very first date.

Because MJ was not a glamorous character, Zendaya dressed casually and wore no makeup for her audition. She auditioned for the part in front of producers Amy Pascal and Kevin Feige. Pascal later said she was blown away by Zendaya's performance, wondering where this amazing actress had come from. Later, Pascal learned that Zendaya was already well-known.

Zendaya's next step was a second audition with Tom Holland, the young British actor who had played Spider-Man in the 2016 film *Captain America: Civil War.* Holland was set to reprise the role in the new movie. The audition was a chemistry read, in which producers would see how well the two actors clicked with one another.

When the actors first met, Holland was nervous. During their first encounter, he could not decide whether to hug Zendaya or shake her hand. Later, Holland joked in an interview, saying it wasn't his smoothest moment. But when Zendaya and Holland began performing their first scene, the incredible chemistry between them was clear. Long before the audition was over, Holland was convinced the producers had found their MJ.

Jon Watts, the director of *Homecoming*, was also excited about Zendaya joining the cast. He had seen her in *K. C. Undercover.* But when Zendaya first auditioned for MJ, Watts did not recognize her because of her casual look. After shooting *Homecoming*, Watts called Zendaya "an amazingly technical actor." He said, "It makes me feel like such a bozo when I'm in front of someone who is that young and already just so good at what they do."[5]

ZENDAYA AND TOM

Once production on *Homecoming* was complete, Zendaya was sent on an international press tour in anticipation of the film's 2017 release. The tour required Zendaya and Holland to spend a lot of time together as they discussed the movie with reporters. The strong affection between the actors quickly became obvious. Holland gushed about how hardworking and professional Zendaya was, while Zendaya called Holland one of the nicest people she had ever met.

Rumors spread that the costars were secretly dating, with one anonymous source telling *People* magazine that they had gone on several vacations together. Determined to keep her private life private, Zendaya joked on social media. She wrote that she found it funny when people said she and Holland went on vacations together, because she hadn't been on a vacation in years.

WATCHING *SPIDER-MAN* TOGETHER

In 2024, several years after Zendaya and Tom Holland made their romantic relationship public, Holland told a reporter that they frequently rewatched *Spider-Man: Homecoming*. Viewing the first film they made together was a way to reminisce about meeting each other when they were 19. Holland said it felt like a luxury to be able to relive their youth through the film.

Spider-Man: Homecoming features a star-studded cast, with Zendaya and Tom Holland appearing alongside actors such as Robert Downey Jr., Michael Keaton, and Marisa Tomei.

Zendaya and Holland's 2017 appearance on the television show *Lip Sync Battle* added fuel to the romance rumors. On the show, celebrities competed to see who could do the best lip-sync performance of a pop song. Each performance was staged as a big production number with backup dancers, sets, and costumes. In Zendaya's number, she lip-synced to the Bruno Mars song "24K Magic." She perfectly mimicked Mars's appearance in the song's music video, which depicts the singer and his friends partying in Las Vegas, Nevada. Wearing red silk pajamas, a gold medallion, and oversized sunglasses, Zendaya matched Mars's swagger as she strutted among showgirls and male dancers. She even rained dollar bills on Holland's head. The crowd went crazy, and Zendaya smiled, confident that she had won the battle.

At first, Holland's performance was comparatively mellow. He lip-synced the song "Singing in the Rain" and performed a dance made famous by actor Gene Kelly in the classic film of the same name. But then Holland rushed behind a curtain of umbrellas, where he shed his coat and suit and emerged wearing a corset, vinyl shorts, and fishnet tights.

The costume change shocked everyone, including Zendaya. Holland, a trained dancer, then performed a daring, spirited lip-sync rendition of the Rihanna song "Umbrella."

During the *Spider-Man: Homecoming* press tour, Zendaya and Holland were frequently seen laughing and goofing around together.

The memorable performance not only won him the lip-sync battle but went viral online.

THE GREATEST SHOWMAN

Zendaya's second movie released in 2017 was a musical titled *The Greatest Showman.* A passion project of actor Hugh Jackman, the film tells the story of P. T. Barnum, the owner of an 1800s circus that features a troupe of talented misfits. Zendaya plays Anne Wheeler, a trapeze artist who falls in love with Phillip Carlyle, a rich playwright portrayed by fellow Disney Channel alumnus Zac Efron.

The role gave Zendaya the chance to show off not only her acting skills but also her singing and dancing skills. But she was first attracted to the project because of the stunt work it involved. Zendaya later recalled feeling excited about the trapeze skills she would have to learn for the part.

Before auditioning, Zendaya met with the film's songwriters, Benj Pasek and Justin Paul. They had worked on the hit Broadway musical *Dear Evan Hansen* and the Oscar-winning film *La La Land*. Zendaya asked to make a recording of her singing Anne and Phillip's big number, a duet titled "Rewrite the Stars." When Zendaya played it for the film's director, Michael Gracey, he was impressed

When Zendaya's character, Anne Wheeler, first appears on-screen in *The Greatest Showman*, she wears a pink wig and purple costume.

by her vocal range. After a brief meeting with Efron, the part was hers.

Before filming, Zendaya and Efron spent several weeks rehearsing. For "Rewrite the Stars," they immediately had problems making the transition from speaking dialogue to singing the song. Pasek and Paul were struggling to make the transition feel more natural when Zendaya suggested that Efron sing the first two lines of the song a cappella. Then the musical accompaniment would start.

Considering themselves the musical theater experts in the room, Pasek and Paul initially dismissed her suggestion. But soon, they realized Zendaya was on to something. When they began the song Zendaya's way, everything clicked into place. Pasek shared the story with MTV News, concluding, "Zendaya . . . you are the queen of all things. . . . You should be doing our jobs, too."[6]

The hardest part of filming "Rewrite the Stars," however, was the stunt work. After being hoisted up by ropes, Zendaya and Efron had to dance high in the air in a circus tent. Zendaya spent weeks training on a rig with a safety net below it. But when she got to the film set, the rig there was 15 feet (4.6 m) taller, and there was no net in sight.[7] Zendaya stood frozen with fear for a moment before costar Hugh Jackman walked by and offered some words of encouragement. That was all the actress needed to get her courage back.

> **"I think something that many actors have, which is something you learn, is that you can't be afraid to look stupid, you can't be afraid to mess up, you can't be afraid of anything."**[8]
>
> —Zendaya, 2021

In one of their most complicated dance moves, Zendaya and Efron had to hold on to ropes and swing far away from each other. Then they had to swing back, grab each other with their free hands, and twirl in the air. The maneuver was tricky. If either actor fumbled the grab, their bodies slammed together. Efron was impressed by how Zendaya handled their many painful collisions. He said, "While I was wincing in pain and covering myself in Tiger Balm and KT tape, Zendaya would move to her next scene completely unfazed."[9]

When *The Greatest Showman* hit theaters in December 2017, the movie industry declared it a dud. The film made only $8.8 million in its first weekend, which was far below expectations.[10] But many moviegoers who saw the film loved it. They told their friends about it and often went back to theaters to see the film again.

The Greatest Showman turned into an unexpected success, eventually earning $469 million worldwide.[11] Zendaya's back-to-back appearances in the blockbuster *Spider-Man: Homecoming* and the surprise hit

WINDING DOWN AT HOME

When Zendaya was in her early 20s, Law Roach often tried to get her to go out at night and have fun like many other college-aged youths do. But when Zendaya leaves a set, she usually prefers to go home and spend time alone to recharge. In her free time, the actress often listens to true crime podcasts or watches movies. After particularly stressful days, she enjoys unwinding with her favorite films, such as the *Harry Potter* movie series.

In *The Greatest Showman*, Anne and Phillip's romantic relationship is threatened by societal expectations about class and race. In "Rewrite the Stars," the pair sings about their feelings for each other.

The Greatest Showman gave her career an enormous boost. Once dismissed as a Disney kid, Zendaya was now a full-fledged movie star.

CHAPTER SIX

STRETCHING HER WINGS

After filming *The Greatest Showman*, Zendaya returned to *K. C. Undercover* to complete the series' final episodes. Going back to Disney Channel after appearing in Hollywood blockbusters was disorienting for the actress. Zendaya said it was "kind of like going to college and then having to go back and do the same grade over and over again."[1]

Zendaya had a new movie project lined up as soon as *K. C. Undercover* wrapped, but suddenly the movie deal fell apart. For the first time since she was 13, she did not have a job. Instead of enjoying some unexpected time off, Zendaya felt panicked and unsure about what to do next.

Zendaya's character, Rue, narrates each episode of *Euphoria*, providing voice-over commentary on the show's events and characters. Zendaya has described Rue as an unreliable narrator. >>

THE WORLD OF RUE

Determined to find work, Zendaya sat down with a pile of scripts for movies and television shows. She usually hated reading scripts because she found them hard to finish without getting distracted. But when Zendaya started reading the pilot script for *Euphoria*, a new TV show on the premium cable channel HBO, she could not put it down.

Based on a 2012 Israeli television drama, *Euphoria* is about students at a California high school who struggle with serious issues, such as violence, drugs, mental health problems, and dangerous sexual situations. At the story's center is its narrator, Rue Bennett, a teenager grappling with drug addiction who begins using drugs again shortly after returning from rehab. After reading the script, Zendaya wanted to play Rue. She knew if she wasn't a part of the show, she'd regret it.

ZENDAYA IS MEECHEE

In 2018, Zendaya voiced the character Meechee, a mythical yeti in the animated film *Smallfoot*. Thanks to a song that went viral on social media, millions knew that Zendaya was Meechee even before seeing the movie. In a 52-second video, comedian Gabriel Gundacker walked past posters for *Smallfoot* and made fun of the characters' goofy names by singing them soulfully, frequently coming back to the line "Zendaya Is Meechee." Over a 24-hour period, more than three million people watched the video on Twitter, including Zendaya.[2] The actress shared it along with three laughing emojis.

In the first season of *Euphoria*, Rue develops a complicated romantic relationship with Jules, who is played by actress Hunter Schafer, *left*.

Zendaya knew she was not the most obvious choice for the role. With her squeaky-clean Disney Channel image, she doubted HBO executives would think she was capable of playing a darker, more mature role. Zendaya also had no direct experience with addiction, calling herself "the most sober person you could ask to play this part."[3] Even so, Zendaya believed she had a lot in common with Rue. "I feel like she's a version of myself with different choices and circumstances," she explained.[4]

When Zendaya met with the series' creator, Sam Levinson, she was shocked to hear that she had been on his mind when he started working on *Euphoria.* While writing the pilot, Levinson had put together a mood board. This is a collection of text and images that creative artists assemble to help them shape the tone of a project they are developing.

One image on his mood board was a photograph of Zendaya. He thought she would be a good fit for Rue, even though she was not familiar with the thoughts and emotions of addiction. Levinson could tell her about that because he had used opiates and methamphetamines for several years before achieving sobriety at age 19.

Despite Levinson's confidence in her, Zendaya felt terrified on her first day on the show's set. She had never played a character like Rue before. She took Levinson aside and asked him to tell her if she was doing a bad job. She told him that she was tough and could handle any criticism he might have. Levinson assured her that he would but said he was not worried about her performance.

SPIDER-MAN: FAR FROM HOME AND *EUPHORIA*

After filming the *Euphoria* pilot, Zendaya spent several months playing a very different high school student. She reprised her role as MJ in *Spider-Man: Far from Home*, the second film in the rebooted *Spider-Man* series. In the

Spider-Man: Far from Home features a stunt scene in which Peter Parker and MJ swing through the air and land on a bridge.

first film, Zendaya's character has only a handful of lines. But in *Far from Home*, she has much more screen time since the plot involves a romantic relationship between MJ and Peter Parker. The movie includes the two characters' first on-screen kiss.

Once *Spider-Man: Far from Home* wrapped, Zendaya returned to the *Euphoria* set to film the rest of the series' first season. Her initial nervousness about playing Rue was gone. Zendaya had formed a tight working relationship with Levinson, who encouraged her and her costars to improvise. The second episode featured an intense scene between Zendaya and Nika King, the actress who plays Rue's mother. In the scene, Rue argues with her mother while trying to leave their house to buy drugs.

During the improvised scene, King pinned Zendaya to the floor to keep her from leaving, and Zendaya started furiously screaming. In an unscripted moment, she fought to get away, stood up, and punched a painting on the wall, scattering glass everywhere. Zendaya then picked up a shard of glass and walked toward her scene partner with such menace that it shocked the crew. After the scene, Levinson left the set and burst into tears. Zendaya had perfectly captured the kind of extreme, violent behavior he had displayed when he was dealing with drug addiction.

The emotional intensity of playing Rue at her worst moments was often difficult for Zendaya. She explained, "Your body doesn't know that the situation isn't real; it's absorbing those things and really going through it."[5] She turned to a therapist to help her deal with the difficult emotions that playing Rue brought to the surface.

RUE'S HOODIE

For many *Euphoria* fans, one of the series' most exciting elements is the costuming. The show's young cast members wear many memorable outfits. But the most iconic piece of *Euphoria* clothing is a simple, oversized burgundy hoodie worn by Zendaya's character, Rue. In the pilot script, Sam Levinson wrote that Rue had a habit of using the hoodie to hide herself as a coping mechanism on bad days. In her own backstory for Rue, Zendaya decided that the hoodie comforted Rue because it had belonged to her recently deceased father.

Zendaya found an upside to her feelings of vulnerability too. She felt that working on *Euphoria* had made her a more emotionally open person. The part also helped her be more courageous when choosing challenging projects. It made her more willing to try new things in her professional and personal life.

Although Zendaya continued to keep her romantic life private, gossip magazines and websites noted that in late 2019, Zendaya was spotted several times with Australian actor Jacob Elordi, who plays Nate in *Euphoria*. People speculated that the costars were dating, although neither actor confirmed the relationship. At the same time, rumors spread that Tom Holland was dating family friend Olivia Bolton. If these relationships were in fact real, rumors concluded that they both came to an end in early 2020.

TOMMY X ZENDAYA

While filming the first season of *Euphoria*, Zendaya was also busy with a fashion-related side project. She and Law Roach partnered with American designer Tommy Hilfiger to create the Tommy x Zendaya collection. At first, Zendaya was hesitant to collaborate with Hilfiger. She feared that his company just wanted to use her name without letting her have any input on the designs.

Zendaya and designer Tommy Hilfiger posed with models at the Fall 2019 Tommy x Zendaya fashion show. It took place in Harlem, New York City.

But after she and Roach presented Hilfiger executives with a mood board of what they had in mind for the collection, the executives quickly embraced Zendaya's ideas.

Zendaya's inspiration was her grandmother's wardrobe from the 1970s. She envisioned a collection of tailored separates, such as pants and blazers, paired with flowy pieces, including skirts, blouses, and dresses. Zendaya insisted that the collection include plus sizes, which was a first for Hilfiger's company.

Tommy x Zendaya was first presented at Paris Fashion Week in March 2019. The fashion show was modeled after the Battle of Versailles, a famous fashion event of 1973, during which American designers emerged as leaders in the world fashion industry. The Battle of Versailles was also the first fashion show to feature a large number of Black models.

All the models in the Tommy x Zendaya show were women of color, including Pat Cleveland, a famous Black model who had walked the runway at the Battle of Versailles. Other models included singer Grace Jones and model Beverly Johnson, who was the first Black woman to appear on the cover of American *Vogue*. For Zendaya, the show was a thrilling way to celebrate the Black women who came before her in the entertainment and fashion worlds.

BECOMING JOAN OF ARC

Zendaya wore one of her most beloved looks at the 2018 Met Gala. The gala's theme was "Heavenly Bodies: Fashion and the Catholic Imagination." Law Roach dressed Zendaya as Joan of Arc, a Catholic martyr who was burned at the stake in the 1400s partially because she wore the armor of a male warrior. Zendaya sported a red bob wig, a dress made of armored plates and sequined chain mail, and silver high heels. She made a splash on the red carpet but immediately had to find a seat because the extremely heavy dress made her feet ache.

CHAPTER SEVEN

BACK TO WORK

In early 2019, Zendaya was thinking about her next step in Hollywood when she heard about an intriguing project—a new film adaptation of the classic science fiction novel *Dune*. The book tells the story of the Atreides family, who manages the mining of a substance known as spice on the planet Arrakis. This desert world is home to giant sand worms.

Zendaya later remembered, "From the beginning, I was just like, 'I'll play a tree, the sand worm. What do you need? This is so cool. I just want to be there.'"[1] In the script, the role best suited to Zendaya was Chani, a mysterious woman of the Fremen, the native people of Arrakis.

In the *Dune* films, Zendaya's character, Chani, has bright-blue eyes and wears futuristic armor. >>

In 2021, Zendaya attended the Venice Film Festival with her *Dune: Part One* costars.

The exciting story wasn't the only thing that attracted Zendaya to the project. She also wanted to be in *Dune* so she could work with the movie's director, Denis Villeneuve. She had seen Villeneuve's 2013 film *Prisoners* and thought he was very talented. Zendaya also wanted to perform with Timothée Chalamet, who had signed on to play Paul Atreides. She had never met Chalamet but admired him as an actor.

During their first meeting, Villeneuve was impressed by Zendaya. He said that at her audition, the actress actually made him believe she was from another planet.

But it was the chemistry read between Zendaya and Chalamet that won her the part of Chani. The two actors instantly clicked. Zendaya could tell that they were going to be good friends.

Villeneuve's *Dune* dramatized only part of the long novel—a section in which Chani barely appeared. Because of this, Zendaya had a minor role in the film. She provided some narration at the beginning of the movie and appeared in several of Paul's visions. But in total, she had only about seven minutes of screen time.[2]

The small role meant that Zendaya was on set for only a short time. The other cast and crew members were already used to working with one another when she arrived, but they welcomed her warmly, and she quickly fit in. Zendaya developed a rapport with Villeneuve, whose thoughtfulness and preparation she appreciated.

He was equally impressed by Zendaya, stating, "I was particularly amazed by the high precision of her acting skills, her intelligence, her graceful patience and her great generosity."[3] Chalamet was also excited to have Zendaya on set because she was the only person there who was his age. The two actors enjoyed joking around with each other and having impromptu dance parties in Zendaya's trailer.

THE COVID-19 PANDEMIC

At the beginning of 2020, Zendaya was looking forward to returning to the *Euphoria* set for the series' second season. But in mid-March, she got a call from Sam Levinson, who informed her that filming was postponed indefinitely because the virus that causes COVID-19 was quickly spreading worldwide. Because of the deadly pandemic, businesses shut down. Many people across the United States were confined to their homes.

Unable to work, Zendaya realized she had to find a way to occupy herself during what seemed like endless free time. Her friend and *Euphoria* costar Hunter Schafer bought her some oil paints, so she tried her hand at painting. But her interest quickly waned. Later, she bought a piano and watched YouTube videos to teach herself

BLACK STYLE

In September 2020, Zendaya was featured on the cover of *InStyle* magazine. For the cover shoot, Zendaya insisted on wearing clothing, jewelry, and shoes created by Black fashion designers, including Jason Rembert and Christopher John Rogers. She knew these designers' creations rarely appeared in national magazines and hoped the exposure would help their businesses. Behind the scenes, all the photographers, hairstylists, and makeup artists involved were also Black. It was *InStyle* magazine's first photo shoot with all-Black creatives.

how to play. But Zendaya did not stick with any of these hobbies. All she wanted was to get back on set, and that seemed impossible.

Soon, Zendaya was fighting off depression. She felt as if she had a dark cloud hanging over her and did not know how to get rid of it. By May, she was sleeping until midafternoon just so she would not have to plan what to do each day. One night, Zendaya decided she had finally had enough. She called Levinson and told him that somehow, they had to find a way to start a new project.

Zendaya proposed shooting something at her house with a cast and crew of just three people—herself, Levinson, and *Euphoria* cinematographer Marcell Rév. The group originally thought about making a psychological horror movie with Zendaya as the only actor. But then Levinson came up with a more ambitious idea. His inspiration was a mistake he had made at the premiere of his 2018 movie *Assassination Nation*, during which he forgot to thank his wife, who was a producer on the film.

> **“I get everything from acting. It’s my social life. It’s my hobby. It’s my fun thing to do. It’s my challenge.”** [4]
>
> **—Zendaya, 2021**

Levinson drew on that situation to create a story about an all-night fight between a director named Malcolm and his girlfriend, Marie, at their home. He quickly wrote the first ten pages and sent them to Zendaya, who loved the story. Having played middle school and high school students for her entire career, she was excited to get her first real adult role.

BEHIND THE CAMERA

Many characters in *Euphoria* endure ugly experiences. But the careful lighting and stylish use of color makes the show look dreamy and beautiful. Zendaya loves how *Euphoria* is photographed by cinematographer Marcell Rév. When she is not in a scene, she likes to watch Rév work and see how he lights different scenes. To learn more about this process, Zendaya took Rév's advice and began experimenting with photography, often using old film cameras.

MALCOLM & MARIE

Levinson titled the film *Malcolm & Marie*. After he finished writing the script, there were several problems to solve before filming could begin. One was finding someone to play Malcolm. Levinson approached *BlacKkKlansman* and *Tenet* star John David Washington, who eagerly accepted the role.

Although the movie involved only two actors and one location, the project still required a small crew. Levinson and Zendaya recruited crew members who had worked on *Euphoria*. In order to start filming as soon as possible, Zendaya and Levinson decided not to seek out investors for the movie. Instead, Zendaya, Levinson,

Washington, producer Kevin Turen, and Levinson's wife, Ashley, put up their own money to cover the movie's $2.5 million budget.[5]

The team's biggest problem was figuring out how to bring together a 22-member cast and crew without exposing anyone to COVID-19.[6] The film was one of the first to be shot during the pandemic, so the crew made up their own rules. These had to be approved by the production's doctors and by the labor unions for film actors, directors, and writers.

After the team gathered at the house that was to serve as the set, they all went into quarantine for two weeks, spending most of their time in their own rooms. Each person was frequently tested for COVID-19, and all rehearsals were held outside in a parking lot. After the quarantine period, filming began. Only 12 people were allowed on set at any time as a precaution.[7]

Over several days in June and July of 2020, the crew filmed *Malcolm & Marie* without mishap. Zendaya was relieved to be back on a set—the one place she always felt most comfortable. As she later recalled, "There were tough days, and it was exhausting. But . . . we created this set family of support."[8] *Malcolm & Marie* was a success on several levels. It proved profitable when Netflix purchased

Malcolm & Marie was shot in black and white to evoke the style of old Hollywood movies.

the movie for $30 million.[9] Zendaya made sure a portion of the profits were distributed among the crew members to thank them for their hard work.

The film's crew also established many COVID-19 protocols that were later adopted by other television and movie productions, helping to keep Hollywood open for business during the rest of the pandemic. Those productions included *Spider-Man: No Way Home*, the third installment of the rebooted Spider-Man franchise, and two special episodes of *Euphoria* that aired between seasons one and two.

One of the episodes features a long, intense conversation between Rue and Ali, her sponsor in her attempt to overcome addiction. Ali is played by acclaimed actor Colman Domingo. In a 2021 interview with Zendaya, Domingo said the special episode was one of the proudest moments of his career.

AN UNUSUAL EMMY AWARDS

Like many other young Black Americans, Zendaya was preoccupied with more than just COVID-19 in the summer of 2020. For years, she had been horrified by a series of highly publicized police killings of Black Americans, such as Philando Castile, Alton Sterling, and Breonna Taylor. Public anger reached its peak with the murder of George Floyd, a Black man in Minneapolis, Minnesota, who died at the hands of the police.

Despite the ongoing pandemic, millions took to the streets to protest Floyd's death as part of the Black Lives Matter (BLM) movement. To do her part, Zendaya invited Patrisse Cullors, who cofounded BLM in 2014, to take over her Instagram platform. There, Cullors could directly explain BLM to Zendaya's followers.

In early September, Zendaya was preparing for the Emmy Awards, the television industry's highest honors. She was nominated for Outstanding Lead Actress in a Drama Series for her role in *Euphoria*. Zendaya felt a little uncomfortable giving so much attention to an awards ceremony when so many young people were protesting in the streets. But the normally glitzy ceremony was to be much more subdued that year because there was no in-person event. To prevent the spread of COVID-19, nominees would appear on the broadcast via computer cameras.

That did not stop Zendaya and Law Roach from putting together a showstopping outfit for the event. On the night of the ceremony, Zendaya wore a glittery silver halter top and a full black skirt with white polka dots. The actress wanted to look sharp even though she expected to be on-screen for only a moment while applauding the winner. She believed her chances of winning the award were slim, given that her competition included famous stars such as Jennifer Aniston, Sandra Oh, and Olivia Colman, all of whom had far more experience in the entertainment industry than she did.

2020 EMMY

When Zendaya was awarded the Emmy for Outstanding Lead Actress in a Drama Series in 2020, she made history. At 24, she was the youngest woman to ever win in that category. She was also the second Black actress to receive the honor. The first was Viola Davis, who won for her role in *How to Get Away with Murder* in 2015.

Zendaya accepted her 2020 Emmy Award during the virtual ceremony broadcast, giving an emotional acceptance speech.

Zendaya nervously watched the ceremony in her living room, surrounded by family and friends. Finally, her category was up. Host Jimmy Kimmel opened the envelope and announced, "And the Emmy goes to Zendaya!" She was stunned for a moment as everyone in her living room cheered. When the noise died down, Zendaya breathlessly praised her fellow nominees and thanked everyone who worked on *Euphoria*.

But she ended her speech with an acknowledgment of BLM protesters. "I just want to say that there is hope in the young people out there," she said. "And I just want to say to all my peers out there doing the work in the streets: I see you, I admire you, I thank you."[10]

CHAPTER EIGHT

A MAJOR STAR

Like many people, Zendaya had a hard time dealing with feelings of uncertainty and isolation during the COVID-19 pandemic. In early 2021, the availability of a COVID-19 vaccine momentarily slowed the pandemic. Zendaya, eager to film and promote new projects, was thrilled to be in the spotlight again.

Zendaya's first movie released in 2021 was *Malcolm & Marie*, which had a brief theatrical run in January before becoming available for streaming on Netflix. The actress's next release was *Space Jam: A New Legacy*, a sequel to the 1996 sports comedy *Space Jam*. Both *Space Jam* films feature live-action basketball stars interacting with animated characters.

At the 2021 premiere of *Space Jam: A New Legacy*, Zendaya wore a colorful outfit inspired by her character in the film. >>

FASHION ICON

In 2021, the Council of Fashion Designers of America (CFDA) honored Zendaya with its annual Fashion Icon Award. At 25, she was the youngest person to ever receive the award. But CFDA executive Steven Kolb noted that despite the actress's young age, she had made a huge impact on style. Zendaya's status as a fashion icon was further bolstered by the spectacular outfit she wore to the ceremony. She appeared in a bright-red, strapless, bandeau-style crop top that exposed her midriff. She paired the top with a matching floor-length skirt that had a poofy peplum at the waist. The look was designed by Vera Wang.

Zendaya's involvement in the film began with a phone call from Ryan Coogler, one of the movie's producers. Zendaya had long wanted to work with Coogler, the Black director of dramas such as *Fruitvale Station* and *Creed*. Before he could tell Zendaya why he was calling, she blurted out that she would likely say yes to whatever he told her.

When Coogler said he had a part for her in a *Space Jam* sequel, Zendaya could not have been happier. Her mother had played basketball in college, and her father had been a high school basketball coach. She had loved the game for as long as she could remember.

Zendaya voices Lola Bunny, the only female animated basketball player in the original film. For *A New Legacy*, director Malcolm D. Lee revamped the character from a flirty girl in a crop top and shorts to a star player who wears the same uniform as the boys. Some *Space Jam* fans were upset by these changes, but Zendaya defended the new Lola Bunny. "She's . . . an incredible player," she said. "I think in this reimagining of who she is, it just leans into that a little bit more, the fact that she's got these skills and she's an MVP."[1]

DUNE AND SPIDER-MAN: NO WAY HOME

After its original December 2020 release date was postponed because of the pandemic, *Dune* finally hit theaters in October 2021. Two years had passed since Zendaya and Timothée Chalamet first met on the *Dune* set. But on their press tour, the actors picked up their friendship right where they had left off. The duo charmed reporters with their genuine rapport and inside jokes as they sang each other's praises. On the TV show *Good Morning America*, Chalamet said, "I'm counting my lucky stars that I've got a

Zendaya chatted with costar Timothée Chalamet while promoting *Dune: Part One* at the 2021 Venice Film Festival. She paired her leather dress with a silver-and-green snake necklace.

friend in this crazy industry that I can count on, and she's got the same here."[2]

Zendaya also received attention for the fashions she wore while promoting *Dune*. One eye-catching look was a leather gown she sported at the Venice Film Festival. Two years earlier, Zendaya had sent Law Roach an image of a dark-brown leather corset from the design house Balmain. She asked whether it could be made into a floor-length dress. Roach worked with Balmain to craft the gown, lightening the color of the leather to match Zendaya's skin tone. Evoking the sand that covered the desert planet in *Dune*, the beige dress clung to Zendaya's body in a way that made it appear as if it was wet.

Two months later, Zendaya was traveling the world on another press tour for *Spider-Man: No Way Home*, the

NOT ENOUGH ZENDAYA

Most entertainment reporters gave Zendaya high marks for her successful publicity blitz of 2021. But Zoe Haylock, a writer for *Vulture*, took issue with how prominently Zendaya appeared in the publicity for *Dune*, given her brief screen time in the film. She said Zendaya deserved bigger parts, but "instead, she's used to create hype for expensive franchises."[3] Haylock's article, titled "Zendaya Is in *Dune* for 7 Minutes," went viral among Zendaya fans on Twitter. Many felt the movie's trailers tricked them into believing the actress had a major role.

During the *Spider-Man: No Way Home* press tour, Zendaya and Holland charmed audiences with their playful banter and natural chemistry. The pair was interviewed alongside costar Jacob Batalon, *left*, in 2021.

third installment of the Spider-Man trilogy. This press tour was different from those for the previous films because Zendaya and costar Tom Holland were no longer hiding the fact that they had resumed their romantic relationship. During the previous summer, paparazzi had snapped photographs of the costars kissing inside Holland's sports car when it was stopped at a red light in Los Angeles.

News outlets published the photos, dubbing the couple "Tomdaya." Zendaya and Holland decided they had to admit they were a couple, as so many fans and reporters had long suspected. For Zendaya, the press's reaction to their romance was unsettling. "It was quite strange and weird and confusing and invasive," she later said.[4]

Once again, Zendaya and Holland won the hearts of the press with their easygoing, affectionate interactions on the press tour. A *Los Angeles Times* reporter went so far as to declare that Holland and Zendaya had stolen the public's heart. Zendaya used the press tour to reflect on the journey that her character, MJ, had taken in the three movies. MJ is a wisecracking sidekick in the first film, a love interest in the second, and a partner in saving the world in the third. Zendaya also talked about how excited she was to meet former Spider-Man actors Tobey Maguire and Andrew Garfield, who both appear in *No Way Home*.

SPIDER FASHIONS

After receiving rave reviews for Zendaya's elegant looks on the Dune press tour, Law Roach promised that the actress's outfits for *Spider-Man: No Way Home* would be more playful. He decided to dress Zendaya in a series of spider-themed outfits. On one red carpet, she wore an oversized Alexander McQueen blazer and boots decorated with jeweled web designs. She accessorized with dangling cobweb earrings. At another event, Zendaya donned a sheer gown with black embroidered web patterns. She wore a matching mask created just for her by designer Pierpaolo Piccioli.

BACK TO *EUPHORIA*

Meanwhile, Zendaya was also busy filming the second season of *Euphoria*. For the first season, she had informally acted as a producer. But for season two, she was given an official producer credit. Zendaya and Sam Levinson worked together to craft an ambitious arc for Rue. Episode five of the season takes Rue to her darkest place yet, with addiction nearly destroying her life.

Playing Rue in such deep distress took an emotional toll on Zendaya. Levinson, who had experienced drug addiction in the past, also found it painful to write about Rue hitting rock bottom. Zendaya sometimes had to go to Levinson's house to calm him down and motivate him to delve into difficult scenes. After completing the episode, the team reworked Rue's story for the rest of the season because they thought the character deserved a more hopeful ending. By the final episode, Rue is sober and actively working to put her life back together.

Despite the season's creative successes, tensions were growing on the *Euphoria* set. The cast and crew complained of long workdays. There were also press reports that Zendaya and Levinson's relationship had become strained. Zendaya was reportedly upset that Levinson was neglecting *Euphoria* and spending more

Euphoria won six trophies at the 2022 Emmy Awards, including Zendaya's Lead Actress award.

time working on *The Idol*, another HBO series. The actress was supposedly concerned enough to call a meeting with network executives. In turn, Levinson was reportedly upset that Zendaya's movie career was taking her attention away from *Euphoria*.

On-set problems, however, had no effect on *Euphoria*'s viewership. Drawing an audience of more than 16 million for each episode, it became the second-most-watched show on HBO after *Game of Thrones*.[5] Zendaya received four Emmy nominations for her work on the show's second season, including for acting, producing, and writing the lyrics for two songs on the show, "Elliot's Song" and "I'm Tired."[6]

Zendaya took home one award, winning her second Emmy for Outstanding Lead Actress in a Drama Series. This time, she accepted the award in an auditorium full of cheering people. In her speech, Zendaya movingly paid tribute to Rue and the viewers who saw themselves in the character: "Anyone who has loved a Rue, or feels like a Rue, I want you to know that I'm so grateful for your stories, and I carry them with me, and I carry them with her."[7]

CHAPTER NINE

GOING FORWARD

When Zendaya first read the script for the 2024 movie *Challengers*, she felt herself drawn to the character of Tashi, a professional tennis player who becomes a coach after suffering an injury. The character gets into a romantic triangle with her tennis-star husband, Art, and her ex-boyfriend, Patrick, a failed tennis player. Tashi intrigued Zendaya, but the actress had some reservations about the role. Zendaya was used to playing fairly sympathetic characters.

Despite Rue's messy life in *Euphoria*, audiences largely felt for the character as she struggled with addiction and depression. But Tashi was different. She was tough, abrasive, controlling, and sometimes

At the 2024 *Challengers* premiere in London, England, Zendaya reunited with costars Josh O'Connor, *left*, and Mike Faist, *right*. >>

TASHI'S T-SHIRT

In the trailer for *Challengers*, Zendaya's character, Tashi, sports a gray T-shirt with the words "I TOLD YA" printed on it in big black letters. The T-shirt became a sensation, especially after Zendaya was seen wearing it in New York City during the film's press tour. The shirt was designed by *Challengers* costume designer Jonathan Anderson, who was director of the brand Loewe at the time. Loewe began selling versions of the shirt in its stores and on its website. Because Zendaya had worn it, other people wanted to wear the shirt too.

manipulative of those close to her. Zendaya was a little scared of Tashi, but she told herself that she couldn't pass up the opportunity to play the character.

Challengers also allowed Zendaya to tackle something new: playing an adult woman with a husband and child. Although much of the film's story is told in flashbacks, including one in which Tashi, Art, and Patrick meet as teenagers, the present-day storyline features Tashi in her early thirties. This was several years older than Zendaya was herself.

The actress was excited about the opportunity to be a producer on *Challengers* too. She helped scout filming locations and select the director, Luca Guadagnino, who had directed Timothée Chalamet in the 2017 hit *Call Me by Your Name*. Zendaya also had the idea of casting Josh O'Connor as Patrick. She admired O'Connor's performance in the television series *The Crown*.

To play tennis pros, Zendaya, O'Connor, and their costar Mike Faist had to spend three months working with a coach.[1] Zendaya knew nothing about tennis and disliked working out, which made the intensive tennis lessons stressful. She quickly grew frustrated, especially on days when she could not even hit the ball over the net.

But eventually, Zendaya realized she did not have to become a good tennis player to look like one, especially because the balls and rackets in the film were to be added later as visual effects. Instead of trying to learn the sport, Zendaya started copying the movements and footwork of her trainers as if she were performing a dance. She said, "If I could do a foxtrot, I think I can learn tennis footwork."[2]

BACK TO *DUNE*

Zendaya's physical training on the *Challengers* set came in handy on her next project, *Dune: Part Two*. This film covered the second half of Frank Herbert's novel, in which Zendaya's Chani has a much more prominent role as the love interest of Chalamet's Paul Atreides. But director Denis Villeneuve wanted to delve even deeper into Chani's conflicted emotions than the book did. While Chani is falling in love with Paul, she must deal with her misgivings as he becomes a cultlike leader to her people.

The role posed several challenges for Zendaya and Chalamet, such as figuring out how young people in a futuristic setting would talk and flirt with each other. But the most difficult part of Zendaya's job involved filming in the deserts of Jordan and the United Arab Emirates. To play a space warrior, Zendaya had to wear heavy armor. She appreciated that her *Challengers* workouts had built up her calves enough so that she could tromp through the sand in her costume without too much effort.

But Zendaya ran into trouble when she ignored reminders to stay hydrated. It took several minutes to get out of her costume to go to the bathroom, so the actress did not drink as much water as she needed. This resulted in a bad case of heatstroke in the desert sun.

Challengers and *Dune: Part Two* were both filmed in 2022 and scheduled for release in late 2023. But because of a strike by the Screen Actors Guild–American Federation of Radio and Television Arts—the labor union representing film and television actors—Zendaya and her costars could not promote the movies if they were released on schedule. Instead, their studios postponed the films' releases until after the strike was settled. Both were rescheduled to hit theaters in the spring of 2024. Meanwhile, back-to-back press tours for *Dune: Part Two* and *Challengers* gave Zendaya a chance to create a series of red-carpet showstoppers, which would dominate celebrity news for months.

BECOMING A DIRECTOR

For years, Zendaya has said that she hopes to become a film director someday. Working toward that goal, she spent much of her time on the *Challengers* and *Dune: Part Two* sets shadowing her directors, learning how they managed their cast and crew. *Challengers* director Luca Guadagnino has encouraged Zendaya to pursue her dream of directing. He told *Vogue*, "She has such a vast curiosity . . . combined with a rigorous discipline and a sort of scientific interest in the technique, I think she would be amazing at it."[3]

DRESSING THE PART

For the *Dune: Part Two* press tour, Law Roach searched for futuristic-looking garments. In Paris, France, Zendaya wore a white dress by the fashion house Alaïa. The gown's unusual cutouts and gold metal embellishments gave it an unearthly vibe. In Seoul, South Korea, the actress donned a vintage Alexander McQueen suit with red detailing that looked like a computer's motherboard. The detailing was filled with liquid that glowed in the dark.

Zendaya's most memorable *Dune: Part Two* look was her own idea. She asked Roach if he could find a famous chrome-and-plexiglass "cyborg" bodysuit that took the fashion world by storm when a model wore it at a

1995 Thierry Mugler fashion show. Roach agreed to track the bodysuit down, but only after Zendaya promised she would wear it no matter how uncomfortable it was.

When Zendaya tried the bodysuit on, it fit perfectly. But within ten minutes, the heat trapped by the metal of the suit almost made her pass out. Refusing to back out of her promise, Zendaya wore the suit to *Dune: Part Two*'s London premiere. According to *Women's Wear Daily*, the social media frenzy over the robotic look generated more than $13 million worth of free publicity for Thierry Mugler.[4]

Zendaya's outfits for the *Challengers* tour were much more comfortable. She donned a variety of outfits evoking the classic uniforms of female tennis players. Other looks featured shades of green inspired by tennis courts and tennis balls. One outfit that created buzz was a sparkly silver tennis dress paired with

Zendaya's showstopping cyborg bodysuit featured clear plexiglass panels and built-in gloves. She accessorized with a diamond necklace and a slicked-back hairstyle.

white shoes, which had tennis balls spiked on their slender metal heels.

> **"I think about red carpets as having their own characters and narratives. . . . It's like an extension of my acting career in a weird way. . . . I get to meet these different women through clothes."** [5]
>
> **—Zendaya, 2021**

Zendaya continued her streak of iconic fashions as a cochair of the Met Gala in May 2024. The gala's theme was "The Garden of Time." Zendaya arrived in a peacock-inspired blue-and-green gown and headdress from the John Galliano design house. To the crowd's surprise, Zendaya made a second appearance on the gala's red carpet. This time, she wore a vintage black taffeta dress from her own closet. The Galliano gown had made its debut in a Givenchy fashion show in 1996, the year Zendaya was born.

ONLY THE BEGINNING

Zendaya created even more buzz when she walked the red carpet at the Golden Globe Awards in January 2025. She was nominated for Best Performance by a Female Actor in a Motion Picture—Musical or Comedy for her role in *Challengers*. The actress epitomized Hollywood glamour in a burnt-orange, strapless Louis Vuitton gown and a short, wavy hairstyle. Roach crafted the look as a tribute to Joyce Bryant, a Black nightclub singer of the

At the 2024 Met Gala, Zendaya's blue-and-green gown featured intricate details such as clusters of grapes and a hummingbird.

1940s and 1950s. The look was stunning, but Zendaya's fans were drawn to one accessory—a ring with a large diamond on her left ring finger. Rumors that Zendaya and Tom Holland were engaged flooded the internet and were soon confirmed through the couple's family and friends.

It looked like a Hollywood ending for the couple. But Zendaya's success in building a loving partnership amid the pressures of living in the public eye had nothing to do with movie magic. Instead, it had everything to do with the actress's own determination. Even while emerging as one of the greatest stars of her generation, Zendaya has worked hard to maintain her privacy and to nurture relationships away from the spotlight. That same determination has allowed Zendaya to develop an A-list career on her own terms. She has chosen projects with care, seeking work that satisfies her creative spirit and allows her to collaborate with passionate artists.

One of the most eloquent statements about Zendaya was written by *Dune* director Denis Villeneuve. It was published in *Time* magazine, which named Zendaya one of its 100 Most Influential People of 2022. Villeneuve wrote, "She is timeless, and she can do it all. . . . A cultural icon in the making. A person driven by pure inspiration, empathy, and respect for her craft, who uses authenticity as a new superpower. . . . Zendaya is the future. . . . This is only the beginning."[6]

FUTURE PROJECTS

By late 2024, two years had passed since Zendaya had been on a television or movie set. Afraid that her acting skills were rusty, she told *Vanity Fair* that she wasn't sure she could do it anymore. But that fear did not stop her from taking on a host of new projects. By early 2025, Zendaya had signed on to appear in three movies, *Dune: Messiah*, *The Drama*, and *The Odyssey*. She was also set to voice a character in the animated film *Shrek 5* and to reprise her role as Rue in season three of *Euphoria*.

ESSENTIAL FACTS

Full Name: Zendaya Maree Stoermer Coleman

Date of Birth: September 1, 1996

Place of Birth: Oakland, California

Parents: Claire Stoermer; Kazembe Ajamu Coleman

Education: Graduated from Oak Park High School in Oak Park, California, after studying with a tutor on set

RISE TO STARDOM

- At age 13, Zendaya moved to Los Angeles, California, to become a professional performer. She was cast as a colead in the Disney Channel show *Shake It Up*.
- Zendaya appeared in two Disney Channel movies and starred in another Disney Channel series, *K. C. Undercover*, which she helped produce.
- In 2016, Zendaya was cast as MJ in *Spider-Man: Homecoming*, which launched her movie career. She reprised the role in two more films in the franchise.

CAREER HIGHLIGHTS

- Zendaya starred in several nonfranchise movies, including *The Greatest Showman*, *Malcolm & Marie*, and *Challengers*, for which she received a Golden Globe nomination.
- For her role in the television series *Euphoria*, Zendaya won the Emmy for Outstanding Lead Actress in a Drama Series in 2020 and 2022.

- Zendaya was awarded the 2021 Council of Fashion Designers of America Fashion Icon Award and served as a cochair of the 2024 Met Gala.

MAJOR TV SHOWS AND FILMS

- *Shake It Up* (2010–2013)
- *K. C. Undercover* (2015–2018)
- *Euphoria* (2019–)
- *Spider-Man: Homecoming* (2017)
- *The Greatest Showman* (2017)
- *Malcolm & Marie* (2021)
- *Dune* (2021)
- *Dune: Part Two* (2024)
- *Challengers* (2024)
- *Dune: Part Three* (2026)

QUOTE

"I get everything from acting. It's my social life. It's my hobby. It's my fun thing to do. It's my challenge."

—Zendaya, 2021

GLOSSARY

a cappella
Sung without musical accompaniment.

acclaimed
Enthusiastically praised.

alumnus
A former member of a school, group, or organization.

animosity
A feeling of dislike, resentment, or hostility.

cinematographer
A member of a film crew who oversees photography and camerawork.

fashionista
A person who is knowledgeable and enthusiastic about fashion.

franchise
A series of stories and associated media and products that share a setting, a story, or characters.

impromptu
Not planned or rehearsed.

improvise
To make up dialogue and actions for a character on the spot without a written script.

pandemic
An outbreak of disease over a large area.

paparazzi
Photographers who take pictures of celebrities and sell them to media outlets.

quarantine
A state or period of isolation, often to prevent the spread of a disease.

rapport
A friendly, understanding relationship or connection.

reboot
To revive a movie franchise or television series.

red carpet
An event before an awards show where performers or celebrities show up in gorgeous attire, get photographed, and do interviews.

reprise
To repeat a performance or a song.

stereotype
An oversimplified or unfair idea about a particular group of people.

vulnerability
An openness that leaves one at risk of being hurt physically or emotionally.

ADDITIONAL RESOURCES

SELECTED BIBLIOGRAPHY

Brown, Laura. "Zendaya Is Entering Her Boss Phase." *InStyle*, 12 Oct. 2021, instyle.com. Accessed 21 Jan. 2025.

Hirschberg, Lynn. "Zendaya Leans into the Chaos of Her Characters." *W*, 3 Jan. 2025, wmagazine.com. Accessed 24 Jan. 2025.

Marius, Marley. "Zendaya Talks *Challengers*, Talks *to* Serena Williams, and Considers Her Future." *Vogue*, 9 Apr. 2024, vogue.com. Accessed 21 Jan. 2025.

FURTHER READINGS

Hämeenaho-Fox, Satu. *A to Zendaya: A Celebration of a Pop Culture Icon*. DK, 2023.

Lapointe, Tanya, and Stefanie Broos. *The Art and Soul of Dune: Part Two*. Insight Editions, 2024.

Marvel's Spider-Man: No Way Home the Official Movie Special Book. Titan Comics, 2023.

Mooney, Carla. *Tom Holland*. Abdo, 2026.

ONLINE RESOURCES

To learn more about Zendaya, please visit **abdobooklinks.com** or scan this QR code. These links are routinely monitored and updated to provide the most current information available.

MORE INFORMATION

For more information on this subject, contact or visit the following organizations:

THE COSTUME INSTITUTE AT THE METROPOLITAN MUSEUM OF ART

1000 Fifth Ave.
New York, NY 10028
metmuseum.org/departments/the-costume-institute

The Costume Institute at the Metropolitan Museum of Art in New York City houses and conserves 33,000 pieces of clothing and accessories dating from the 1400s to the present. The annual Met Gala is a benefit for the institute. Zendaya has worn several amazing outfits to this event.

THE WALT DISNEY FAMILY MUSEUM

104 Montgomery St.
San Francisco, CA 94129
waltdisney.org

The Walt Disney Family Museum features exhibits about Walt Disney's life and work. The company he founded later established the Disney Channel, which gave Zendaya her first big break.

WARNER BROS. STUDIO TOUR HOLLYWOOD

3400 Warner Blvd.
Burbank, CA 91505
wbstudiotour.com

The Warner Bros. Studio Tour Hollywood offers tours of Warner Bros. film studios. Guests can explore the WB Archive Museum, which features props, costumes, and photographs from movies such as Zendaya's *Dune* films.

SOURCE NOTES

CHAPTER 1. BECOMING ZENDAYA

1. "2015 Academy Awards, Kevin Hart and Zendaya on Oscar Red Carpet." *YouTube*, uploaded by BlackTree TV, 22 Feb. 2015, youtube.com. Accessed 16 June 2025.

2. Lauren Waterman. "2015 Is the Year of Zendaya." *Teen Vogue*, 5 Jan. 2015, teenvogue.com. Accessed 21 May 2025.

3. "Zendaya: Five Facts." *BBC*, 21 Sept. 2020, bbc.com. Accessed 21 May 2025.

4. Alessandra Codinha. "Zendaya Is This Academy Awards' Breakout Style Star." *Vogue*, 22 Feb. 2015, vogue.com. Accessed 21 May 2025.

5. "Giuliana Rancic Makes 'Weed' Comment about Zendaya." *YouTube*, uploaded by Today's Internet Sensation, 15 June 2018, youtube.com.

6. Alexandra Perron. "Singer Zendaya Calls Out Giuliana Rancic for Offensive Hair Comments." *Yahoo!*, 24 Feb. 2015, yahoo.com. Accessed 21 May 2025.

7. Genevieve Field. "The Unstoppable Zendaya." *Glamour*, 9 Feb. 2016, glamour.com. Accessed 21 May 2025.

8. Perron, "Singer Zendaya Calls Out Giuliana Rancic."

9. Field, "The Unstoppable Zendaya."

10. Natalie Stone. "Giuliana Rancic Makes Somber On-Air Apology to Zendaya." *Hollywood Reporter*, 24 Feb. 2015, hollywoodreporter.com. Accessed 21 May 2025.

11. Hilary Lewis. "Zendaya Responds to Giuliana Rancic's Apology." *Hollywood Reporter*, 25 Feb. 2015, hollywoodreporter.com. Accessed 21 May 2025.

12. Nicole Spector. "Zendaya Barbie Honors Star for 'Standing Up for Her Culture.'" *Today*, 29 Sept. 2015, today.com. Accessed 21 May 2025.

CHAPTER 2. GROWING UP

1. Allison Takeda. "Zendaya Gets to the Heart of Her Family Tree for Immigrant Heritage Month." *Us Weekly*, 8 June 2015, usmagazine.com. Accessed 21 May 2025.

2. Sylvia Obell. "Zendaya on Winning Her Emmy, Activism through Art." *Essence*, 6 Dec. 2020, essence.com. Accessed 21 May 2025.

3. Lynn Hirschberg. "Zendaya Leans into the Chaos of Her Characters." *W*, 3 Jan. 2025, wmagazine.com. Accessed 21 May 2025.

4. Lynn Hirschberg. "Zendaya Is Next, Next, Next!" *W*, 9 Mar. 2016, wmagazine.com. Accessed 21 May 2025.

5. Genevieve Field. "The Unstoppable Zendaya." *Glamour*, 9 Feb. 2016, glamour.com. Accessed 21 May 2025.

6. Clover Hope. "Zendaya Holds Court." *Elle*, 23 Aug. 2023, elle.com. Accessed 21 May 2025.

7. Lauren Waterman. "2015 Is the Year of Zendaya." *Teen Vogue*, 5 Jan. 2015, teenvogue.com. Accessed 21 May 2025.

8. Yara Shahidi. "Zendaya on Blackness, Beyoncé, and Telling Disney 'No.'" *Glamour*, 2 Oct. 2017, glamour.com. Accessed 21 May 2025.

9. Char Adams. "Zendaya on Cameo in Beyoncé's Lemonade." *Essence*, 26 Oct. 2020, essence.com. Accessed 21 May 2025.

CHAPTER 3. A DISNEY KID

1. Lauren Waterman. "2015 Is the Year of Zendaya." *Teen Vogue*, 5 Jan. 2015, teenvogue.com. Accessed 21 May 2025.

2. Bill Gorman. "Disney Channel Original Movies in Development." *TV by the Numbers*, 16 June 2011, web.archive.org. Accessed 22 May 2025.

3. Justin Shady. "Duo 'Shake' Up Disney." *Variety*, 22 Oct. 2010, variety.com. Accessed 22 May 2025.

4. "'Shake It Up' Canceled." *HuffPost*, 25 July 2013, huffpost.com. Accessed 22 May 2025.

5. Shady, "Duo 'Shake' Up Disney."

6. Jack Irvin. "Zendaya Doesn't Know If She 'Could Ever Be a Pop Star.'" *People*, 7 June 2022, people.com. Accessed 22 May 2025.

7. Brenton Blanchet. "Everything Zendaya and Val Chmerkovskiy Have Said about Their Partnership." *People*, 3 Jan. 2025, people.com. Accessed 22 May 2025.

8. Suzan Clarke. "'Dancing with the Stars' Results." *ABC News*, 22 May 2013, abcnews.go.com. Accessed 22 May 2025.

9. Clarke, "'Dancing with the Stars' Results."

10. Lynn Hirschberg. "Zendaya Leans into the Chaos of Her Characters." *W*, 3 Jan. 2025, wmagazine.com. Accessed 21 May 2025.

11. Hirschberg, "Zendaya Leans into the Chaos of Her Characters."

12. Marley Marius. "Zendaya Talks Challengers, Talks *to* Serena Williams, and Considers Her Future." *Vogue*, 9 Apr. 2024, vogue.com. Accessed 22 May 2025.

CHAPTER 4. TAKING THE REINS

1. Abby Aguirre. "Zendaya Talks Spider-Man, Her First Love, and Reinventing Disney Stardom." *Vogue*, 15 June 2017, vogue.com. Accessed 21 May 2025.

2. Kathryn Shattuck. "Zendaya Doesn't Need a Safety Net." *New York Times*, 15 Dec. 2017, nytimes.com. Accessed 22 May 2025.

3. "nooncolemann." *Instagram*, n.d., instagram.com. Accessed 22 May 2025.

4. Yara Shahidi. "Zendaya on Blackness, Beyoncé, and Telling Disney 'No.'" *Glamour*, 2 Oct. 2017, glamour.com. Accessed 21 May 2025.

5. Shahidi, "Zendaya on Blackness, Beyoncé, and Telling Disney 'No.'"

6. "K. C. Undercover." *IMDb*, n.d., imdb.com. Accessed 22 May 2025.

7. Lisa Hiser. "Zendaya Gets Tough for Teen Vogue." *Shine On Media*, 6 Jan. 2015, shineon-media.com. Accessed 22 May 2025.

8. Vrinda Jagota. "Seeing Red: Zendaya to the Extreme." *Paper*, 3 June 2019, papermag.com. Accessed 22 May 2025.

9. Jagota, "Seeing Red."

10. Lynn Hirschberg. "Zendaya Leans into the Chaos of Her Characters." *W*, 3 Jan. 2025, wmagazine.com. Accessed 21 May 2025.

11. Shahidi, "Zendaya on Blackness, Beyoncé, and Telling Disney 'No.'"

12. Genevieve Field. "The Unstoppable Zendaya." *Glamour*, 9 Feb. 2016, glamour.com. Accessed 21 May 2025.

SOURCE NOTES

13. Field, "The Unstoppable Zendaya."

CHAPTER 5. BREAKOUT

1. Kathryn Shattuck. "Zendaya Doesn't Need a Safety Net." *New York Times*, 15 Dec. 2017, nytimes.com. Accessed 22 May 2025.
2. Constance Grady. "What Makes Zendaya a Great Celebrity." *Vox*, 15 July 2019, vox.com. Accessed 22 May 2025.
3. Tatiana Siegel. "Zendaya Responds to 'Spider-Man' Casting Controversy." *Hollywood Reporter*, 9 Nov. 2016, hollywoodreporter.com. Accessed 27 May 2025.
4. Siegel, "Zendaya Responds to 'Spider-Man' Casting Controversy."
5. Abby Aguirre. "Zendaya Talks Spider-Man, Her First Love, and Reinventing Disney Stardom." *Vogue*, 15 June 2017, vogue.com. Accessed 21 May 2025.
6. "Zendaya Is 'The Queen of All Things.'" *YouTube*, uploaded by MTV News, 19 Dec. 2017, youtube.com. Accessed 16 June 2025.
7. "Zendaya Shows One of Her and Zac Efron's Trapeze Fails." *YouTube*, uploaded by The Tonight Show Starring Jimmy Fallon, 12 Dec. 2017, youtube.com.
8. Colman Domingo. "Zendaya Tells Colman Domingo How She Found New Purpose." *Interview*, 7 Dec. 2021, interviewmagazine.com. Accessed 27 May 2025.
9. Aguirre, "Zendaya Talks Spider-Man."
10. Dana Schwartz. "The Greatest Showman Has Almost Titanic-Length Legs at the Box Office." *Entertainment Weekly*, 27 Feb. 2018, ew.com. Accessed 27 May 2025.
11. "The Greatest Showman (2017)." *Box Office Mojo*, n.d., boxofficemojo.com. Accessed 27 May 2025.

CHAPTER 6. STRETCHING HER WINGS

1. Phoebe Reilly. "Zendaya Jumps from Disney to Drug Binges in HBO's Graphic 'Euphoria.'" *New York Times*, 13 June 2019, nytimes.com. Accessed 27 May 2025.
2. Marina Pedrosa. "Zendaya Is Loving the 'Zendaya Is Meechee' Meme." *Billboard*, 24 Sept. 2018, billboard.com. Accessed 27 May 2025.
3. Marisa Meltzer. "'There's So Much I Want to Do': The World According to Zendaya." *British Vogue*, 6 Sept. 2021, vogue.co.uk. Accessed 27 May 2025.
4. Reilly, "Zendaya Jumps from Disney to Drug Binges."
5. Laura Brown. "Zendaya Is Entering Her Boss Phase." *InStyle*, 12 Oct. 2021, instyle.com. Accessed 22 May 2025.

CHAPTER 7. BACK TO WORK

1. Rebecca Keegan. "'Who Am I When I'm Not Working?'" *Hollywood Reporter*, 3 Jan. 2025, hollywoodreporter.com. Accessed 27 May 2025.
2. Jack Smart. "How Dune: Part Two Expands Zendaya's Role." *People*, 2 Mar. 2024, people.com. Accessed 27 May 2025.
3. Marisa Meltzer. "'There's So Much I Want to Do': The World According to Zendaya." *British Vogue*, 6 Sept. 2021, vogue.co.uk. Accessed 27 May 2025.

CONTINUED. . .

4. Pamela McClintock. "'I Was So Desperate to Work.'" *Hollywood Reporter*, 2 Mar. 2021, hollywoodreporter.com. Accessed 27 May 2025.

5. McClintock, "'I Was So Desperate to Work.'"

6. Gina Cherelus. "Zendaya on 'Malcolm & Marie' and That Toxic Relationship." *New York Times*, 21 Feb. 2021, nytimes.com. Accessed 27 May 2025.

7. Anthony D'Alessandro. "Reopening Hollywood." *Deadline*, 8 July 2020, deadline.com. Accessed 27 May 2025.

8. Kate Aurthur, "Zendaya Goes Deep on the Making of 'Malcolm & Marie.'" *Variety*, 26 Jan. 2021, variety.com. Accessed 27 May 2025.

9. Aurthur, "Zendaya Goes Deep on the Making of 'Malcolm & Marie.'"

10. "72nd Emmy Awards: Zendaya Wins for Outstanding Lead Actress in a Drama Series." *YouTube*, uploaded by Television Academy, 20 Sept. 2020, youtube.com.

CHAPTER 8. A MAJOR STAR

1. Derek Lawrence. "Zendaya Talks Voicing 'Iconic' Lola Bunny." *Entertainment Weekly*, 12 July 2021, ew.com. Accessed 27 May 2025.

2. Christi Carras. "Could Timothée Chalamet and Zendaya Be Any More Charming?" *Los Angeles Times*, 22 Oct. 2021, latimes.com. Accessed 27 May 2025.

3. Zoe Haylock. "Zendaya Is in Dune for 7 Minutes." *Vulture*, 22 Oct. 2021, vulture.com. Accessed 27 May 2025.

4. Oliver Franklin-Wallis. "Tom Holland Is in the Center of the Web." *GQ*, 17 Nov. 2021, gq.com. Accessed 27 May 2025.

5. Kim Masters. "What's Ailing 'Euphoria'?" *Hollywood Reporter*, 23 July 2024, hollywoodreporter.com. Accessed 27 May 2025.

6. "Zendaya." *Television Academy*, n.d., televisionacademy.com. Accessed 27 May 2025.

7. Matt Grobar. "Zendaya Again Sets Emmy Record." *Deadline*, 12 Sept. 2022, deadline.com. Accessed 27 May 2025.

CHAPTER 9. GOING FORWARD

1. Clover Hope. "Zendaya Holds Court." *Elle*, 23 Aug. 2023, elle.com. Accessed 21 May 2025.

2. Lynn Hirschberg. "Zendaya Leans into the Chaos of Her Characters." *W*, 3 Jan. 2025, wmagazine.com. Accessed 21 May 2025.

3. Marley Marius. "Zendaya Talks Challengers, Talks *to* Serena Williams, and Considers Her Future." *Vogue*, 9 Apr. 2024, vogue.com. Accessed 22 May 2025.

4. Hannah Malach. "Zendaya's 'Dune' Premiere Robot Suit Generates $13.3 Million for Mugler." *Women's Wear Daily*, 26 Feb. 2025, wwd.com. Accessed 27 May 2025.

5. Laura Brown. "Zendaya Is Entering Her Boss Phase." *InStyle*, 12 Oct. 2021, instyle.com. Accessed 22 May 2025.

6. Denis Villeneuve. "Zendaya." *Time*, 23 May 2022, time.com. Accessed 27 May 2025.

INDEX

ABOUT THE AUTHOR

LIZ SONNEBORN

Liz Sonneborn, a graduate of Swarthmore College, has written more than 120 books for young readers and adults on a variety of subjects. Her specialties include US history, world history, biography, women's studies, and African American studies. Sonneborn is a longtime resident of Brooklyn, New York.